Enduring Through the Storms
"A BIBLICAL PERSPECTIVE ON SUFFERING IN THE WORLD"

Clarence Benoit III

COPYRIGHT © 2009. Clarence Benoit III

Enduring Through the Storms
by Clarence Benoit III

ISBN 9781615796830

All rights reserved solely by the author. The author guarantees all contents are original and do not infringe upon the legal rights of any other person or work. No part of this book may be reproduced in any form without the permission of the author. The views expressed in this book are not necessarily those of the publisher.

Unless otherwise indicated, Bible quotations are taken from the New International Version of the Bible. Copyright © 1973, 1978, 1984 by the International Bible Society. Used by permission of Zondervan Publishing House. All rights reserved.

Surely he took up our infirmities
And carried our sorrows,
Yet we considered him stricken by God,
Smitten by him, and afflicted.

But he was pierced for our transgressions,
He was crushed for our iniquities;
The punishment that brought us peace
Was upon him,
And by his wounds we are healed.

We all, like sheep, have gone astray,
Each of us has turned to his own way;
And the Lord has laid on him
The iniquity of us all.

(Isaiah 53:4-6)

Table of Contents

Acknowledgments 5

Introduction 7

Chapter 1: So, What Happened? 11

Chapter 2: Why Does Suffering Persist? 27

Chapter 3: Is God Doing Anything About It? 181

Chapter 4: Now What? 229

References 279

ACKNOWLEDGMENTS

A sincere thanks to Charlie Sawyer, Clyde King, Harold Oliver Sr., Mark Lindsay, Maurice Hooks, and Robert Milner who contributed their time, effort, thoughts, and much-needed encouragement to help me bring this book to completion. Throughout my years as a disciple, it's been the various qualities that I've seen in you all such as the selflessness, humility, friendships, wisdom, genuine love for those around you, and faithfulness that has collaborated to help encourage and strengthen me in my walk with God. It's an honor and a blessing to serve with such faithful men of God. I can't tell you how much I appreciate the example you set in speech, in life, in love, in faith, and in purity. May God continue to bless you in all of your endeavors.

A special thanks to Amanda Lapierre who generously took the time out of her busy schedule to assist with proofreading and providing feedback. In just the short time that I've known you, you've been very encouraging to me. I am grateful to have met you, and it's a pleasure having you as a friend. Your sincerity and genuineness are refreshing. I pray God pours out an abundance of blessings on you and your family. Thank you!

Introduction

uffering, in its many forms, is probably one of the most widely used aspects of life manipulated to discredit the existence of God and all of the glorious virtues of His nature. Many individuals have turned from the faith to atheism claiming that there absolutely cannot be a god with all of the death and suffering that's so prevalent in the world we live in. Others remain in total confusion about the whole issue. They waiver between the concepts of whether

God is omnipotent, but not good or that God is good, but not omnipotent. They question how can a loving God allow so much suffering in the world, sit back, and do absolutely nothing about it. As we go about our daily lives and observe all of the afflictions such as poverty, crimes, accidents, abuse, disease, war, natural disasters, and terrorism just to name a few, it is so obvious that suffering is a natural part of the world we live in. Yet, due to our nature, we refuse to accept and deal with it as we should. We want things to be easy and comfortable, yet a life like this would provide no benefit for us under the current circumstances. Here are a few simple facts that we must come to know and understand. First, there is a reason for all of the suffering that we see in the world and there is a specific purpose in each of our afflictions, whether it is revealed to us or not. Second, there isn't any single answer to our suffering and there is no escape from it. Lastly, suffering has no place in our concept of life, but that must change. You might ask what we need to do about it. It is imperative that we gain a biblical view of the purpose of suffering so that we may have the right perspective, which will lead to a more appropriate response when we're staring affliction straight in the eyes. This is especially true of disciples because we have been commissioned to be ambassadors of Christ, His examples to the world, a responsibility we fully accepted when we came to know Him. Despite this, we are not exempt from having the same views of suffering as someone who doesn't know Jesus Christ. As a result, this can cause us to sway dangerously in our faith and keep us from standing firm in our convictions and our relationship with God. With that in mind, you have to ask yourself this question. How are you going to make a difference in the world for Jesus Christ if you're behaving the same way they do towards one of the most abundant and relatable experiences in life? From what I've learned through the Scriptures and experience, mine, as well as the experience of others, I will address the following questions. Why is there death and suffering in the first place? Why does God purposely allow death and suffering to persist in the world? And, is God doing anything about it? Also, as you begin to read through this book, I would suggest you perform a little self-analysis by asking yourself these questions. Do you have any unresolved trials lingering in your heart? Is there something that you've conveniently forgotten about or stuffed in the closet because you didn't want to deal with it? I hope that you would pull those experiences out of the closet and attend to them as you read through this book. You might just find yourself on the path to getting some closure about the experience and a sense of peace.

CHAPTER ONE

So, What Happened?

efore I delve into the subject matter, I'd like to get an obvious fact of life out of the way. By design, God created us with the ability to decide on our own what we want to do completely independent of any outside influence. Quite naturally, what I'm referring to here is free will. Free will is the essence of humanity. Without it, we'd be nothing more than mere robots and that's not what God desired for us because He desired to have a relationship with

His most prized creation. He would love us and we would choose to love Him in return. So, you ask, what does free will have to do with anything? Well, let's take a look into the Scriptures and see how it fits into what actually happened.

Traveling back to the beginning, let's take a look at a few Scriptures in Genesis, which literally means the origin or beginning of something. When God finished creating all that He had made, it was considered to be very good (Genesis 1:31). After God created Adam, He placed him in the Garden of Eden without any restrictions except the one. He was told that he mustn't eat of the tree of the knowledge of good and evil (Genesis 2:17) for when he ate of it, he was guaranteed to die. Death, which did not exist at this point, was the penalty for disobeying God's command; it was never a part of God's original plan. In Genesis 3:6-7 is where we see the impact of one man's free will, not only on himself but on every human being to come after him. Here, Adam disobeyed God's only command and in Genesis 3:19, we see God executing His judgment, thus, bringing death and suffering into the world because of sin. This should give us all some indication as to the current ability of man to maintain a position of obedience before God. There was one and only one command that God gave for Adam to be concerned about. The command, if I must say, was rather simple in nature, nothing too complicated about it at all. Not to mention the fact that God gave Adam free reign to eat of any of the other trees that were in the garden. You would think that all of those other trees would have been enough to keep Adam occupied and keep his attention off of that one tree. Oh, but no! That one tree became the focal point. As sin wasn't in the world, Adam didn't have a sinful nature to struggle with or the knowledge of good and evil, which would make him responsible for moral discernment. Adam, along with every man to come from him, gained that when he ate of the tree that he wasn't supposed to eat. All he had to do was do what God told him to, enjoy life and his relationship with God, and that would have been the end of that. It seems like a simple task, but Adam chose to do what God told him not to do. Adam was fully aware of what he had done (Genesis 3:8-12, I Timothy 2:14). Then, to make matters worse, instead of simply taking responsibility for his own actions, he indirectly blames God for it all by placing blame on the woman that God had given him. Knowing the character of God, I believe things would have been vastly different than they are now if Adam would have taken responsibility for his error. These facts are essential in helping us to understand who's at fault here for all of the death, pain, and suffering that are going on in the world. The fault rests with man, not God. Do you hear what I am saying? Believe it or not, there are people who blame God, as Adam did in the beginning, for all of the agonies that's going on in their lives. In reality, if they only obeyed God, they would be alleviated from many of the unnecessary sufferings and would be far better off in their lives. Now, don't misconstrue what I just said into life would be perfect and easy because that's definitely not the case here. Remember earlier that I said there is a purpose for suffering, which will be discussed later.

What were the implications of Adam's disobedience to God's command? What was the message that was being sent? When Adam rebelled (sinned) against God, essentially what he was telling God is that he wanted life without Him, which is impossible because God is the source of all life and to be without God is to be without life. He also told God that he wanted to decide truth, what's right and wrong, for himself. Anyone with young children should understand this concept of disobedience all too well. How many times have you told your child not to do something like playing in the middle of the street? Then, no sooner than you turn your back, where do you see your child? Playing in the middle of the street!

Now, you've explained to them why they shouldn't be in the street along with its dangers and the consequences. Is this not what God did with Adam? Was not Adam somewhat like your little child? We can see the impact that Adam's actions had long term on all of mankind from the following Scripture.

> [12]Therefore, just as sin entered the world through one man, and death through sin, and in this way death came to all men, because all sinned – [13]for before the law was given, sin was in the world. But sin is not taken into account when there is no law. [14]Nevertheless, death reigned from the time of Adam to the time of Moses, even over those who did not sin by breaking a command, as did Adam, who was a pattern of the one to come.
>
> (Romans 5:12-14)

Therefore, since we are all descendants of Adam, the first man from whom all other men came, we inherited his problem. We sin "in" Adam or more appropriately; we sin after the likeness of Adam. This means, with the exception of Christ, of course, that all of mankind by nature rebel against God. We choose to do what we want to do when we want to without any regard to our Creator and His moral standards. Therefore, the consequence we face is eternal condemnation. This is what so many people have a problem with. They say if God is a loving god, then how could He condemn someone eternally to hell? This doesn't exemplify love and is definitely not a characteristic of a loving god. Therefore, they conclude that God must not be a loving god or that God will not send them to hell. This grants them permission to continue in their wickedness. On the contrary, the wrath of God against sin and the wickedness of man are in perfect alignment with His loving nature, which we will briefly discuss in just a few seconds. Sin is destructive thereby making every evil act that man commits against each other (which is ultimately against God) an absence of love (Romans 13:8-10). If you watch the news or read the daily newspaper, you have come to familiarize yourself with the evidence. Rape, murder, abuse, adultery, theft, molestation, what else do you need, the list goes on. God can't coexist with wickedness and His action to destroy sin and anything associated with it is in perfect harmony with His nature because sin is in stark contrast to His. If He accepted anything even slightly less than this, then this would contradict His nature. God wouldn't be perfect. God wouldn't be holy. God wouldn't be good. God wouldn't be love. God, simply, wouldn't be God. The truth is the very fact that we would even ask such a question exposes more so the severity of man's depravity. We not only tolerate sin, but we indulge ourselves, take pride in it, and find great joy and encouragement when others take part in all of the filth with us. Yet, we have the audacity to find it unfathomable and bring God's character into question when He completely abolishes it from His presence. Well, the truth is that we can't understand it because we're the ones who are unloving and have fallen so very short of the intentions God had for us in the beginning. Paul was expressing this same point when he wrote to the church in Rome when he sought to help the Jewish Christians there see that they were in the same boat as the Gentile Christians, whom they had an issue with having to share in God's grace with (Romans 1:18-20, 2:1-4, 3:21-24).

So, how did God respond to this deliberate act of disobedience? In addition to judging sin with death, God gave us just what we asked for. He gave us a taste of life without Him by removing some of His sustaining power. Colossians 1:15-17 tells us that

> [15]He is the image of the invisible God, the firstborn over all creation. [16]For by Him all things were created: things in heaven and on earth, visible and invisible, whether thrones or powers or rulers or authorities; all things were created by Him and for Him. [17]He is before all things, and in Him all things hold together.

This Scripture makes it clear that all things are held together by the power of God, our Creator the Lord Jesus Christ. Since He removed some of His sustaining power, all things are not held together as perfectly as God is capable of doing. If you want to see an example of God holding things together perfectly, refer to Deuteronomy 29:5 and Nehemiah 9:21. As the Israelites wandered throughout the desert for 40 years, God held them together so much so that their shoes and clothing didn't wear out. I can't help but imagine what life in this world would have been like before sin's entrance and God holding every single detail of it together like this. All of His sustaining power has not been removed because if it were, the entire creation would cease to exist. Romans 8:20-22 says,

> [20]For the creation was subjected to frustration, not by its own choice, but by the will of the one who subjected it, in hope [21]that the creation itself will be liberated from its bondage to decay and brought into the glorious freedom of the children of God. [22]We know that the whole creation has been groaning as in the pains of childbirth right up to the present time.

Because sin entered the world, the entire creation is suffering as a result. The world has been subjected to pain, frustration, and decay. Simply put, we live in a fallen world. The fact that God is giving us somewhat of a taste of what life would be without Him explains why there is so much violence, death, and disease in the world and why things are only getting worse from generation to generation. This is what happens when we decide to make our own decisions completely in opposition to God's will. In getting this small taste of life without God, we should all be running to God for refuge and His gracious gift of salvation. But, due to our sinfulness, we are so blinded to the truth that we cannot see what's really going on. This act of God removing some of His sustaining power reminds me of a saying I first heard years ago. It states, "For a true Christian (*someone living as a disciple*), this life is the closest that they'll get to hell and for a non-Christian, this life is the closest they'll get to heaven". In light of these Scriptures, I believe that this is absolutely true because hell, in summary, is total separation from God. So, if you think things in this lifetime are bad, just wait till you get a load of the next if you leave this world without properly accepting Jesus as your Lord and Savior.

God had demonstrated this type of judgment on other occasions over the course of history. As we briefly look at Romans 1:18-32, we see Paul writing to the church in Rome, specifically the Jewish disciples, regarding the spiritual condition of the Gentiles over the course of history. He makes it clear to them that the Gentiles knew God but chose not to glorify or give Him thanks. They exchanged the glory of the one true immortal God for images created by man. They decided to follow a lie instead of the truth of God; in doing so, God abandoned them over to such wickedness and depravity as an act of judgment and a display of His wrath. This is a spiritual predicament that should be avoided at all costs. Living with the knowledge of God and His truth, rejecting it to the extent that God completely abandons you over to the many lusts of your heart, only for you to suffer in this life, then pass from this world into an eternity of condemnation all because of a lie you would not let go of. Another example of when God gave the people what they wanted despite His warnings of what was going to happen comes from the following passage.

> ⁴So all the elders of Israel gathered together and came to Samuel at Ramah. ⁵They said to him, "You are old, and your sons do not walk in your ways; now appoint a king to lead us, such as all the other nations have." ⁶But when they said, "Give us a king to lead us," this displeased Samuel; so he prayed to the LORD. ⁷And the LORD told him: "Listen to all that the people are saying to you; it is not you they have rejected, but they have rejected me as their king. ⁸As they have done from the day I brought them up out of Egypt until this day, forsaking me and serving other gods, so they are doing to you. ⁹Now listen to them; but warn them solemnly and let them know what the king who will reign over them will do."
>
> (I Samuel 8:4-9)

As we see from this excerpt of Scripture, the Israelites were asking Samuel to appoint a king to lead them. In doing so, they were rejecting the King that they already had, the LORD God Himself. They wanted a human king because they wanted to be like all of the other nations. As God's people, they were supposed to be different, separated in their desires from the rest of the world. It is so easy to look at this situation with the Israelites and think, what in the world were they thinking? But, that very thought shows the true depth of how much we ourselves are deceived about our very own hearts. I mention this because how often do we struggle with the desires of wanting to partake in the ways of the world, thus, abandoning our relationship with God (I John 1:15-17)? Ever since the fall of man, we have been consistently rejecting, forsaking, and turning away from God. As you proceed to read verse 10 through the end of the chapter of I Samuel, you'll see that they demanded the appointment of a king over them even after God's solemn warning of every single malicious detail of what the king will do to them. Although God knew that this would be a disaster, He gave them just what they had asked for. Why did God allow this and not just protect them? Sometimes, God will give us exactly what we ask for even when He disagrees with it. This doesn't make sense you say. Well, let's take a look at it from a different perspective. The nation of Israel had forgotten all that God had done for them. In essence, they had become prideful. They allowed their hearts to become enticed by the lifestyle of the other nations' and they were no longer submissive to or humble before their God. If they would have been rescued, it wouldn't have done any good in the long run. They would have been left totally oblivious to their condition, which would have only perpetuated their bad behavior (Proverbs 19:19). So, God allowed them to have what they wanted, to suffer the consequences of their actions, and when they would finally realize the mess they were in, they would come running back to Him as He knew they would do (v18). Doesn't this sound like God was teaching His people a lesson? So many times, we can become so hard-headed and prideful that we have to learn things by way of the "School of Hard Knocks." This holds true even when we have someone who is warning us of the consequences we will face if we make a particular decision. Most likely, they are warning us because they've made the same mistake themselves and they love us enough to not want to see us make the same mistake. Let's just face this one simple fact; many times, we just flat out refuse to listen despite the multitude of warnings we may receive.

Once we see our foolishness, how quickly are we to run to God? How eager are we to surrender and humble ourselves before Him?

Chapter Two

Why Does Suffering Persist?

The place where you must start at if you want to even begin understanding why death and suffering persist in the world extends from what I mentioned earlier. We live in a fallen, cursed world. The world is fallen due to the sin that entered the world through one man's rebellion, therefore, causing the world to fall short of the glory that God originally intended for it to have. Cursed because it is under the penalty of sin, which means there are consequences to suffer. As I mentioned earlier, God has given us free will as a part of humanity. It continues to play a part in the suffering that's prevalent in the world because we are imperfect beings who have fallen short of the glory of God. Suffering does persist due to the bad decisions we choose to make in our lives, our own sin, the sin of others, and simple human error. Sin is a harsh reality that we must gain a deep conviction about. It is burdensome, it separates, it destroys relationships, and it's running rampant in the world and in each of our lives. The following Scriptures give a great indication of the severity of sin.

> [13]Your eyes are too pure to look on evil; you cannot tolerate wrong. Why then do you tolerate the treacherous? Why are you silent while the wicked swallow up those more righteous than themselves?
>
> (Habakkuk 1:13)

Then, there's this one.

> [1]Surely the arm of the LORD is not too short to save, nor his ear too dull to hear. [2]But your iniquities have separated you from your God; your sins have hidden his face from you, so that he will not hear. [3]For your hands are stained with blood, your fingers with guilt. Your lips

> have spoken lies, and your tongue mutters wicked things.
>
> (Isaiah 59:1-3)

As the prophet Habakkuk questions God about His decision to use the more wicked Babylonians to punish the nation of Israel, he gives us some insight into God's demeanor towards sin. He absolutely cannot look upon sin. God is so pure and holy that by His very nature, He cannot accept it nor does He possess the ability to tolerate it. For us, this means that we cannot stand in the presence of God in all of our sins. The excerpt from Isaiah 59 tells us the exact result that our sin has on our relationship with God. That relationship is destroyed; we become separated from Him because, as I mentioned earlier, He cannot coexist with wickedness. It's not that God can't save us. It's because we continue in our sin, so He doesn't save us. If you profess to be a Christian, then you need to think about these questions. Do you know what sin is? More specifically, do you know what your sin is? What is your life characterized by, sin or righteousness? Don't flatter yourself. You must be truthful. This is very important. We have to learn to take responsibility for our own malicious decisions that cause suffering in our own lives as well as the lives of others. We need to stop blaming God for everything as alluded to in Proverbs 19:3. In our pride, ignorance, and lack of taking responsibility, it is quite obvious that mankind doesn't realize the absurdity in blaming God for our problems. In the book of Deuteronomy, while Moses reiterated the giving of the Law with the hopes of its true meaning hitting home with the Israelites, he says in chapter 6 verses 1 through 3:

> [1]These are the commands, decrees and laws the LORD your God directed me to teach you to observe in the land that you are crossing the Jordan to possess, [2]so that you, your children and their children after them may fear the LORD your God as long as you live by keeping all his decrees and commands that I give you, and so that you may enjoy long life. [3]Hear, O Israel, and be careful to obey so that it may go well with you and that you may increase greatly in a land flowing with milk and honey, just as the LORD, the God of your fathers, promised you.

At the heart of God's desire for us to obey His commands is that He wants us to enjoy a long life and that things will go well with us. Just think how much better the world would be if people were more apt to obeying God's commands. Just imagine how many problems would dramatically decline or cease to exist if there wasn't so much immorality in the world. I'm referring to problems such as teen pregnancy, sexually transmitted diseases, unwed single mothers (there are some single fathers out there too), and child molestation, along with the many other issues brought about by this sin. Imagine a society with a low murder rate simply because people decided to obey God and value the life of others instead of killing one another. God gave us His precious Laws so that we would have great lives, relationships, and prosper in all the things that He has given us. He is the author of life, so don't you think He would know how it should be lived? We need boundaries and limitations set in order to have this. Just think if we didn't have this, we would literally destroy one another. Imagine driving on our streets and highways without any speed limits, stop signs, and the many other devices used to keep us in line. Let me assure you that this is a chance I'm not willing to take. We already have a hard enough time driving with the devices in place let alone trying to maneuver around without them. Now, that's what I call true love. If you have a hard time accepting the fact that boundaries are necessary, then, I suggest you take a nice long, hard look at Romans 13:8-10. The Law and love go hand in hand; one does not exist without the other.

Although much suffering in the world is provoked directly by the sins of individuals such as the terrorist attacks on the World Trade Center and the massacre at Columbine High School, all suffering is not a direct correlation of a particular individual's sin. Yet, it still is a consequence of sin in general. The types of sufferings that are referred to in these circumstances are things such as disease, poverty, hunger, and natural disasters. A perfect example of this would be the earthquake in the Indian Ocean on December 26, 2004, which caused a tsunami that devastated the landmasses that surround the Indian Ocean. That event produced a loss of more than 230,000 people in approximately a dozen countries. Catastrophic events such as this leave us questioning why. Have you ever viewed a poverty-stricken society and questioned why or how come I've been given so much while they have so little? Or, have you not even given it a thought? Trying to understand these events from merely the human point of view can be pretty perplexing. They can seem senseless, cruel, and downright inhumane. That's why it's imperative that we gain the right perspective from the right source, the Word of God, in order to help us in our understanding. Don't misinterpret this to mean that we'll come to understand everything because we won't. It's impossible! Our limited human minds can't begin to fully understand all the workings of God and what He does, how He does it, and why. But, He does give us some insight into what He does want us to know, that is if we sincerely take the time to search the Scriptures to find out. God does have a purpose in everything He does or allows to happen. That's God's omniscience at work. Well, pain and suffering are no different. There's a purpose in that too. Suffering is just a fact of life that we have to deal with and don't make the mistake of thinking that becoming a Christian is an escape from suffering because you're going to be highly disappointed. Suffering is a significant part of Christianity. As a matter of fact, you may suffer more or in ways you never thought you would. As Christians, we are expected to live in opposition to our own nature. It's seen all throughout the Bible, and Jesus warns us that anyone who chooses to follow Him will suffer. Just take a look at the calling of the apostle Paul in Acts 9:15-16 where Jesus tells Ananias that Paul (then Saul) is His chosen vessel to take His name before the Gentiles and that He was going to show him how much he must suffer for His Name. And, as you read Paul's letters, you'll come to realize that Paul embraced the suffering in his life all the more as he lived out his life for the Name. He had gained such an extraordinary understanding of the suffering in his life that it drastically changed how he viewed it and his whole attitude towards it. Paul's attitude towards suffering was on the opposite end of the spectrum compared to the rest of the world. He was able to see how God was working in his life through that suffering and maintained his focus on that. This is an example we shouldn't hesitate to adopt. I'll now share some of the purposes I've learned about this interesting tool of God and how He uses it to shape our character to bring about a change in our lives for our benefit and His glory. This list is in no way comprehensive nor does it touch on all of the ways that we can be impacted by trials and tribulations. These areas serve merely as a starting point to enlighten you so that you can gain a new perspective. This is beneficial because you will be more likely to progress through and properly deal with difficulties that really challenge you instead of curling up in a ball and calling for mama.

Spiritual Growth

Out of all of God's purposes for allowing suffering that I discuss that directly benefit us, I believe that spiritual growth is the most significant of them all. I believe that because the essence of true Christianity is becoming like Jesus Christ, God's ultimate purpose for our lives (Romans 8:29). Many Scriptures encourage you to "be like Christ" and Jesus calls us to follow Him (Mark 1:17-18). Continual spiritual growth is a monumental aspect of having and maintaining a relationship with God. As we grow closer to God, we trust Him more. Our faith and reliance upon Him increase too. We become more obedient, stronger in our ability to resist the temptation to sin plus a multitude of other blessings as a result of growing spiritually.

> [6]In this you greatly rejoice, though now for a little while you may have had to suffer grief in all kinds of trials. [7]These have come so that your faith – of greater worth than gold, which perishes even though refined by fire – may be proved genuine and may result in praise, glory and honor when Jesus Christ is revealed.
>
> (I Peter 1:6-7)

In the above passage, we see one-way suffering is used in helping us to attain the spiritual growth that God desires for us. We face trials and tribulations specifically for the purpose of testing our faith. The value of our faith is an exceptionally significant aspect of our relationship with God. As the Scripture says, without faith it is impossible to please God (Hebrews 11:6). As a matter of fact, you could say that without faith, you have no relationship with God whatsoever because a lack of faith indicates disbelief in His existence no matter whether that's demonstrated by word or deed. Trials and tribulations will determine the genuineness of our faith, which will be seen in how we respond to the trials we are facing. If we respond in the proper way, obedience towards God, it will bring praise, honor, and glory to God. As I think about this Scripture, I can't help but think about our good ole buddy Job. He was a blameless and upright individual whom God was pleased to acknowledge as one of His own (Job 1:8), yet Job suffered immensely. In Job's suffering, there is something that is particularly noteworthy to consider when we look at our own sufferings. Take note of the fact of who incited God against Job in the first place (v9)? Mind you, this was not done against God's will, but in accordance with it. An important aspect of God's will does include the testing of our faith because He desires that we always remain faithful to Him. Now, don't confuse testing with temptation (James 1:13). God does not tempt; Satan does that. Our faith must be put to the test so we can see where we're at. If we fail, we must refrain from thinking that it's final. This is not true with God. When we fall into the trap of thinking this way, any possibility of growth is lost. I am convinced that through our failures, we can achieve the greatest amount of spiritual growth. This is true only if we avoid the things that prevent us from doing so, learn from it, repent, and allow God to work through us. Continuing on with my point from Job, everything in heaven and on earth, in the physical realm, as well as the spiritual, is under submission to the Almighty. Satan could not have caused the slightest of problems for Job if God hadn't granted him permission (1:12, 2:6, Luke 22:31). At times when you are standing firm in the faith or doing well spiritually and calamity befalls you without any logical explanation; it would be a good idea if you wouldn't be so quick to look at the physical realm for answers. We must remember that there is a spiritual realm for which we do not see any of the activities that are taking place. With every fiber of my being, I do believe that there lies the answer to some of the suffering that takes place in our lives. There is a spiritual battle going on for which we do not see. If we weren't meant to give this some consideration, God would not have allowed us to witness this extraordinary behind-the-scenes event regarding Job that was totally oblivious to him. God never clued Job into what had happened prior to or why he was suffering the trials that he was stricken with despite his persistence in questioning Him. As a matter of fact, Job's questioning of God began to display a lot of self-righteousness. Job seemed as though he was interrogating God in a court of law (Job 10, 13), demanding his due justice. I believe at that point, Job had clearly forgotten who the servant was and who the Master was. Instead of answering Job's questions directly, God had some questions of His own that He posed to Job (Job 38-41). Rhetorical in nature, these were questions that Job in no way, shape, or form could possibly even come close to answering. As a matter of fact, no human being could ever answer questions like those. As I read through the questions that God posed to Job, I couldn't help but be taken aback as I can imagine Job was. I get a more vivid, although not comprehensive, image of God from the questions because it serves as a reminder of His power, wisdom, majesty, and reminds me exactly who the Boss is around here. I think this is the point that God was making to Job, which Job clearly got (Job 42:1-6). Job was instantly humbled. I think God's response to Job was awesome, and I couldn't imagine having it directly told to me by God Himself. In the midst of confusion and the absence of an answer, Job was still expected to live with the integrity that God desired. Just look at how God commends Job before Satan for maintaining his integrity after Satan's first attack (Job 2:3). The lesson for us is no different. We may not ever come to understand why we have suffered what we have in many instances, but you better believe that we are always expected to live with the integrity that God so desires.

> [7]Be patient, then, brothers, until the Lord's coming. See how the farmer waits for the land to yield its valuable crop and how patient he is for the autumn and spring rains. [8]You too, be patient and stand firm, because the Lord's coming is near......... [10]Brothers, as an example

> of patience in the face of suffering, take the prophets who spoke in the name of the Lord. ¹¹As you know, we consider blessed those who have persevered. You have heard of Job's perseverance and have seen what the Lord finally brought about. The Lord is full of compassion and mercy.
>
> (James 5:7-11)

A couple of other aspects of spiritual growth that we can learn from Job's suffering are patience and perseverance. The apostle James admonishes the recipients of his letter to be patient in the midst of suffering because they have the pleasure to look forward to the coming of the LORD. In the same fashion, we should be patient in the midst of our suffering because, in the long-term, we have the exact same hope that the recipients of James' letter had. But in the short-term, we also know that the LORD will faithfully answer us in the midst of our sufferings. So, we should learn to be patient, trust in Him, knowing that He'll answer. As the farmer waits for his valuable gift of crops produced by his land, we should patiently wait for our valuable gift from the LORD as we experience trials. James encourages us to persevere as Job did through his suffering with our primary focus being on what God will bring about through our suffering. Although I wouldn't say that Job was the most patient individual through his suffering, he definitely displayed a noteworthy level of perseverance. By persevering through our trials and tribulations, God will surely bless us richly. In what way remains to be seen, but we have to believe this because that's where the motivation to get through the trials comes from. Look at how much God blessed Job (Job 42:10-17). The LORD blessed Job with twice as much as he had before he suffered. Perseverance through suffering does equate to blessings from God. Remember always that the LORD is gracious and full of compassion and mercy.

Another important aspect of spiritual growth we acquire from suffering is that we are "being made perfect." What exactly does this mean? Especially since no mere human being is or can ever become perfect. What does this passage equate to? This phrase actually refers to us being made more mature. Take a look at this Scripture from the book of Hebrews regarding the perfection of our LORD Jesus pertaining to His sufferings.

> [8]Although he was a son, he learned obedience from what he suffered [9]and, once made perfect, he became the source of eternal salvation for all who obey him and was designated by God to be high priest in the order of Melchizedek.
>
> (Hebrews 5:8-9)

This passage of Scripture had me rather baffled for some years in regard to its practical application and what it meant by "once made perfect", especially since it was made in reference to our already perfect Lord. I had heard an idea or two from a couple of sermons that provided me with some insight, but I wasn't totally convinced that I really understood the depth of what this Scripture was saying. At the unlikeliest moment, I caught a glimpse of what that passage meant. It happened one day while I was hanging out with a friend of mine. We were at practice for one of his teams in his boys' basketball club. On occasion, I would assist in coaching the kids, but that day, I was definitely just hanging out. I was wearing my championship ring from my days of playing college basketball. As I gazed at my ring, the thought of Jesus learning obedience from what He suffered just happened to come to mind. At this juncture, I couldn't help but think that this was an unusual time to be thinking about this. I guess whenever God decides to bless you with some insight into His Word; that's not the time to be picky; you just take it and run with it. I began to reminisce about the trials that I endured through the final year of my collegiate career. It was not so much from the grueling practices as the lack of playing time. This was especially painful for me because there was an individual or two that I could have easily been playing in front of. Some of the students on campus were telling me that I should be playing more and even questioning me as to why I wasn't. How do you answer a question like that? I dealt with some frustration as a result and all of the constant questions didn't help either. At one point, I was determined to forgo the rest of my senior year in order to get a head start on the next stage of my life – earning a living. Thanks to a friend who put things into perspective for me, I hung in there. He asked me two simple questions. The first one was, "For the rest of your life, how many opportunities are you going to have to work?" The next question was just like it but in regard to playing college basketball. After that, this case was closed. I decided to stay; besides this was my senior year. What was I thinking? Prior to Christmas break, we were absolutely horrible considering the talent we had on that team. At the break, we had a six and eleven record. After the break, we absolutely rewrote the story. We went on a twelve to one run and eventually won the NAIA District 10 Championship that earned us a spot in the NAIA Division II National Tournament held in Nampa, Idaho. This was no easy feat. We had to go through the reigning District 10 champions. Then, we had to beat the current conference champions in their own gym. They had already beaten us twice that year rather handily and pretty much owned the rest of the conference. My school hadn't been to the national tournament in forty-two years. Imagine what it was like just being a part of that. That small town was already very proud of their little college and during this time, it only escalated. Because I persevered through this personal trial, I was able to receive a prize that I would have otherwise missed out on. What did I learn from this? Unbeknownst to me, I was learning a lesson in submission and selflessness, two things that are required before the concept in Hebrews 5:8 can even become real. I submitted myself to the coach even though it hurt me by not being involved as much as I probably should have. And, in becoming selfless to a higher cause, eventually, I was able to gain a far greater prize in the end. After the fact, I was so glad that I had stayed. Being able to participate in the national tournament was an experience that I'll never forget. By the way, did I forget to mention that the head coach had been an assistant coach at Washburn University in 1988, the year they won the national championship? My pride and selfishness almost cost me one of the best experiences of my life as an athlete. After coming to this sudden epiphany standing there on the basketball court, I went home and studied into this passage of Scripture a bit more and came to the following conclusion. In stating the obvious, Jesus knew beforehand that He would have to suffer greatly and die on the cross. But, did you ever think, what if Jesus had decided that He wasn't going to go through with it? Of course, you know He did have a choice in the matter of it all and would have been justified if He had decided not to go through with it. To shed some light on the "once made perfect" part, Jesus didn't become "perfect," although He did live a perfect life, until He actually experienced what He already knew He had to go through. Experience is the keyword here to understanding this Scripture. Jesus learned by the actual experience, through obedience to God's will, what His suffering would entail for all of mankind. In bringing His task to completion, Jesus received His just reward. Did you get that? I don't think you did. Let me rephrase that another way. Jesus profited from His sufferings. That's right! Jesus profited from what He suffered. First, God made Him perfect.

> [10]In bringing many sons to glory, it was fitting that God, for whom and through whom everything exists, should make the author of their salvation perfect through suffering.
>
> (Hebrews 2:10)

God perfected Jesus by making Him the One and only who was fully qualified to carry out His mission. Secondly, Jesus, once made perfect, received the right to become the source of eternal salvation for all who would make the choice to obey Him and was designated by God to be the Great High Priest over all who would follow Him. What's the practical application for us? You can only truly understand something when you actually experience and endure it for yourself. That is absolutely the only way. As we face different trials in our lives, being obedient to God (the necessity), we become more mature or "perfect" and stronger in character. This is our great reward from experiencing trials and tribulations. God, no doubt, wants us to be happy and filled with joy, but He is more concerned about our character. This reminds me of an excellent quote I heard years ago that resonated with me. It states:

> The ultimate measure of a man is not where he stands in moments of comfort and convenience, but where he stands at times of challenge and controversy.
>
> (Dr. Martin Luther King, Jr.)

It is extremely easy for us to display good characteristics when things are going good for us and seem to be going our way, but what happens to us when trials come; we tend to crumble, complain, and struggle to no end. When things are great, it's easy to stand firm, but the true measure of our character comes when we face trials. How can we claim to be a loving, patient, compassionate, and humble person when those qualities haven't even been put to the test? God knows exactly who we are, our strengths and weaknesses alike. He allows us to face trials so that we can see who we truly are with the hopes that we'll make a character adjustment. Due to the dynamics of our character, I believe that each individual is different in that we handle certain types of trials much better than we do others. From my personal experiences and what I've observed in the lives of others, the trials that we'll probably face the most are the ones that we don't handle so well. That would indicate a strong weakness in that area of our character, and I believe that God is trying to point it out to us and give us the opportunity to strengthen our character in that area. This can only be done by facing the very things we typically avoid because God doesn't just miraculously strengthen our character where needed. He puts us in situations where we can practice those characteristics. So, the bad-tempered person in your life; maybe God is trying to teach you patience. How about the extremely needy person that makes you want to run every time you see them coming? Maybe God is trying to teach you how to be selfless and give of yourself. Surely not that unruly person at work who just flat out gets on your nerves. Just the mention of their name sets your blood boiling. Maybe God is trying to teach you how to love the unlovable. After all, He did all of those things for us and so much more. We have to understand that God loves us so much that He's not willing to short change us on anything, but He has our back through thick and thin and always has our best interest at heart (Jeremiah 29:11). Since this is such a vital tool for our spiritual growth, how do we come to deal more graciously with pain and suffering in our lives? I believe the answer to that question lies in the following passage of Scripture.

> ¹Therefore, since Christ suffered in his body, arm yourselves also with the same attitude, because he who has suffered in his body is done with sin.
>
> (I Peter 4:1)

The apostle Peter here advises us to arm ourselves with the attitude of Christ Jesus regarding suffering. What exactly was Jesus' attitude towards suffering? Let's look at a Scripture that's one of many examples of Christ's attitude.

> ²¹From that time on Jesus began to explain to his disciples that he must go to Jerusalem and suffer many things at the hands of the elders, chief priests and teachers of the law, and that he must be killed and on the third day be raised to life. ²²Peter took him aside and began to rebuke him. "Never, Lord!" he said. "This shall never happen to you!" ²³Jesus turned and said to Peter, "Get behind me, Satan! You are a stumbling block to me; you do not have in mind the things of God, but the things of men."
>
> (Matthew 16:21-23)

As you can see from this and many other passages, Jesus was very adamant towards facing His sufferings. He ultimately knew that they were from God, the benefit His sufferings would bring about, and He would not be thwarted from participating in them. Jesus had this attitude because He had the things of God in mind. When we resist trials and suffering, we don't have the things of God in mind, but the things of men. Then, Peter, being who he was, had the audacity to take Christ aside and rebuke Him for it. Pay close attention to how Jesus responds to Peter. In addressing Peter, Jesus spoke directly to Satan, who is actually the one behind Peter's remark to Jesus. Satan wants us to have our worldly perspective of suffering. He wants us to take the easy way out, avoid it like the plague, and not remain faithful to God through it all. Satan will use any means possible to accomplish this, as he tried to do with Peter, because suffering, in accordance with obedience to God, brings about God's holiness in our lives (Hebrews 12:10-11). Satan is extremely opposed to this. Now, referring back to our Scripture from I Peter 4:1, it says, "…because he who has suffered in his body is done with sin". That simply means living the holy life that God calls us to. As disciples of Jesus, suffering is simply an indication that you have renounced your sinful lifestyle. We should expect suffering to be a normal part of our lives because we still have to live in this sinful world, we have declared war against our very own sinful nature, and Satan is relentless in his continuing efforts to provoke us to sin. If this is truly our objective, then we must come to embrace the suffering that takes place in our lives. We should view this as an opportunity for us instead of a detriment. Absolutely preposterous you say! Well, I don't think so! Think about all of the pain we subject ourselves to for outcomes that we desire in the end. What comes to my mind is all of the training and conditioning athletes endure in order to be better in their particular sport. You have to like the means to the end in order to consistently subject yourselves to stuff like that. Personally, I could not have played all of those years of basketball if I did not like or was not willing to endure all of the physical pain I experienced from all of the practices (two, sometimes three a days), the excessive amount of running, not to mention, the belittling from the coaches, and the injuries. Over the years, I've twisted my ankles too many times to count, broken both of them along with a bone in my foot, not to mention my wrist on my right hand, and I've suffered from tendonitis in the knees, which continues to plague me to this very day. Yet, at the age of 37, I still continue to play because I'm just not ready to give it up. Now, don't tell me that God didn't give us some capacity to deal with pain and suffering. Our problem is that we want too much control, and we want to decide what we have to deal with depending on how it's going to benefit us in the end. And this, we demand to know upfront! Otherwise, we want no part of it. When we're in control or rather, more appropriately, think we're in control, is when we make a fiasco of things. Well, I think I'm kind of going off on a tangent here, but hopefully, you get the logistics of what I'm talking about.

Manifests God's Power

This reason is one that reigns supreme above all reasons. For that matter, having God's power manifested, not through just suffering, but in every aspect of our lives should be at the very core of why we live and do what we do. The display of His power through our lives leads to His Name being praised, Him glorified and worshipped. God, and God only, is worthy of such reverence. The problem with mankind is that we sincerely think it's all about us, and we are so mistaken. Let's take a look at an example from Scripture that displays the power of God.

> [1]As he went along, he saw a man blind from birth. [2]His disciples asked him "Rabbi, who sinned, this man or his parents, that he was born blind?" [3]"Neither this man nor his parents sinned," said Jesus, "but this happened so that the work of God might be displayed in his life. [4]As long as it is day, we must do the work of him who sent me. Night is coming, when no one can work. [5]While I am in the world, I am the light of the world." [6]Having said this, he spit on the ground, made some mud with the saliva, and put it on the man's eyes. [7]"Go," he told him, "wash in the Pool of Siloam" (this word means Sent). So the man went and washed, and came home seeing.
>
> (John 9:1-7)

This passage holds some interesting points that are keys to enlightening us in our understanding of suffering. In the days of Jesus, people thought that suffering, no matter the illness or disease, was a direct result of sin. This is made clear by the question asked of Jesus by one of His disciples. Jesus refutes this concept by telling His disciples that sin wasn't the cause of this man's blindness. Furthermore, He tells them that this man is that way so that the work of God might be displayed in his life. Of course, Jesus eventually healed the man of his blindness, so that was God's power being displayed, thus, bringing glory and praise to God. But there's something else that I would like to point out in this Scripture that you might not have thought of. Jesus said that the work of God might be displayed. The word that I'm focusing on here is the word "might." This indicates to me that despite God's omnipotence, there is a chance that God's power may not be effective in our lives. Might is a word of uncertainty and only expresses the possibility or likeliness of something happening and yet Jesus uses this word in conjunction with the power of God, something that is full of certainty and assurance. What, then, is the missing factor? The missing factor is our faithfulness. Despite our suffering, will we be faithful enough to be obedient to God and do as we are asked? Jesus asked the man to go and wash. The man was not healed when Jesus put the mudpack on his eyes. What do you think would have happened if the man had not gone to wash? Would he have received his sight? What would that have said about his faith (James 2:17)? God is known for working through man's faith in order to bring His purposes to fruition. God always does His part, but we don't always do ours. From this passage, I believe that the majority of the suffering we face is in place simply to see how we respond to it. It reveals our character, faith, and the condition of our hearts. What position are you going to take regarding the suffering you experience? Are you going to play the role of the victim and let your pain and suffering run your life? Or, are you going to follow the example of the blind man and obey God even when you do not understand? Jesus came to help us with living life to the fullest (John 10:10). Which position do you suppose you have taken? Do you spend a lot of time complaining about your unpleasant situation, expect special treatment from others, or wallow in self-pity by comparing what others can do and you can't? Those are characteristics of someone choosing to be a victim. You must realize that you do have a choice. In modern times, God's power still and always will be manifested in people's lives in so many different ways. All you have to do is look around you. What immediately comes to mind for me are people who are at a physical disadvantage, missing extremities, but by their faith and determination, they are able to accomplish astonishing feats that you would think only a "physically complete" person could accomplish. They simply refuse to do nothing or be hindered by their disability. And, on top of that, they never complain, wallow in self-pity, or expect special treatment from anybody else. I ran across an article of an extraordinary young man in the USA Today a couple of years ago. You may have heard about him. His name is Bobby Martin.[1] He lives in Dayton, Ohio and plays football for the Colonel White High School Cougars. He's only seventeen years old and plays on defense and special teams. If you haven't heard of him, you're probably wondering by now what's so special about this kid. Well, what's so extraordinary about him is that he was born without any legs yet he is a fearless competitor on the football field. He is full of determination and refuses to let his disability become an excuse. This, in my opinion, is God's power being displayed in someone's life. He wanted something and he had the faith and determination, despite his disability, to go after it. Stories about this young man are plastered all over the Internet. I encourage you to take some time to look him up. I believe that he would be a great inspiration to many.

Now, let's briefly delve into this from a broader perspective. I am specifically speaking about the sovereignty of God. In addition to His absolute power, His sovereignty incorporates into the picture His absolute authority over all things and His absolute freedom to do as He chooses to fulfill His purposes within His creation. When an individual understands and sees the sovereignty of God in the bad circumstances in their life, it will change your whole outlook on life altogether, and you will be able to experience the peace of God which transcends all understanding that Paul mentions to the church in Philippi. This will never become more evident than when in the midst of life-shattering circumstances. There are many great examples of people in the Scriptures who exemplified an understanding of the sovereignty of God in their life. With this in mind, let's venture into the book of

Genesis to take a look at a teenager named Joseph and how he demonstrated this concept of the sovereignty of God. When I first became a disciple of Jesus, I studied out the topic of forgiveness because I had a lack of forgiveness in my heart towards my dad for the way he treated me as a child. Joseph was one whom I had studied. After studying his life, I became rather partial to Joseph because I felt that we both had something in common in that we both were abused as children (Genesis 37:12-28). Joseph's brothers weren't very fond of him at all. In fact, they flat out hated him. This was all caused by Jacob's favor and love of Joseph over his brothers. Now, Joseph was a bit of a dreamer, and he didn't mind sharing his dreams with Jacob and his brothers. They just weren't always so receptive to hearing about his dreams and it caused his brothers to hate him all the more. When the opportunity presented itself, Joseph's brothers decided to kill him. Persuaded by Reuben, they only stripped him of his robe, threw him into a cistern, and then sold him into slavery. From there, Joseph ended up in Potiphar's house where his wife took a strong liking to him. When Joseph rejected the invitation of Potiphar's wife, she lied on him to Potiphar causing him to put Joseph in prison where he spent two years of his life (Genesis 39). What a journey Joseph had. All of this happened because of his brothers' hatred toward him. He surely didn't deserve any of the things that happened to him. After seeing Joseph's value, Pharaoh released Joseph from prison and made him second in command over all of Egypt (Genesis 41:41-57). Quite naturally, while serving as second in command of Egypt, Joseph meets his brothers again. Eventually, the whole family moves to Egypt and after Jacob dies, Joseph's brothers become terrified of him. They think that the only reason Joseph has shown them mercy was because of their father. Now that he is dead, they believe that he will exact revenge on them because of all the bad things they've done to him. I believe Joseph's brothers thought this because this is how they would have acted if the shoe was on the other foot. Sometimes, how we think others will respond to us is really a reflection of our own hearts. Now, how in the world is Joseph going to respond to this? They were pretty horrible to him. After all, they did hate him. They sold him into slavery, which led to a chain reaction of other bad experiences he shouldn't have had or deserved in the first place. Not to mention the fact that he was away from his family for thirteen years. Can you imagine the pain that Joseph must have suffered due to his brothers' actions? After experiencing all of this unnecessary drama, here is how Joseph responded to his brothers when they came before him.

> [19]But Joseph said to them, "Don't be afraid. Am I in the place of God? [20]You intended to harm me, but God intended it for good to accomplish what is now being done, the saving of many lives. [21]So then, don't be afraid. I will provide for you and your children. And he reassured them and spoke kindly to them.
>
> (Genesis 50:19-21)

Mind-blowing! That's all that I can say. What an incredible response! As a new disciple, I was completely blown away by his attitude towards his brothers when I studied this out. How would you have responded if you were in the exact same situation as Joseph having experienced all that he had experienced because of his brothers? I wouldn't have even come astronomically close to his response. As a matter of fact, I didn't. My heart, towards my dad, was literally more like Joseph's brothers when they plotted to kill him. It was full of anger and hatred towards him. Being that my dad considers himself to be like Satan, he likes to hit you, push you, and test you to see how much he can get away with you. So, it's inevitable that you will be insulted or disrespected in some kind of way when you're in his presence. Knowing this, I said that if he and I ever met face to face and he disrespected me, I would kill him. I wouldn't shoot him with a gun or stab him with a knife. My desire was to choke him out of this world. I envisioned looking him straight in the eyes so that there'd be no doubt in his mind who it was and why this was happening to him. Pretty sick and twisted, isn't it? Well, it's true. This is the degree to which I hated my dad for the way he treated me. I thank my God for my relationship with Jesus Christ because I no longer feel this way, and I'm the one who's better because of it. I was only hurting myself. I realized that when you harbor any kind of bitterness towards anyone, they usually don't have any idea of how you feel. If they do know, it's a good chance that they may not even care. When we first talked, I hadn't spoken to or seen my dad in over eighteen years. It was during this conversation that I told him that I forgive him. I, also, told him how I felt, that I had hated him all of those years. He was pretty arrogant about the whole thing. I know this because, in our next conversation, he told me what he thought about me telling him how I had felt about him. He said something to the effect that he thought that was some crazy stuff (not his choice of words) that I felt that way about him. He said all of this as though he was justified in the way he treated me – like he had done nothing wrong. He has even told me a few times that I deserved the way he treated me. A dog, let alone a child, doesn't deserve to be treated anywhere near the way he treated me. But, understand this. When you forgive the way God commands you to forgive, the real beneficiary is you. Someone coined an excellent phrase about forgiveness that I believe fits perfectly. The phrase says that when someone chooses not to forgive someone, it's like they decided to drink poison in hopes that the other person will die. In light of this, I feel compelled to ask you this question. Have you been drinking any poison lately? Maybe you drank some long ago, and now, you're still waiting for that person to die. I encourage you to do whatever it takes to let go of your bitterness. You'll be better off because of it. Now, without Joseph seeing that God was working through all of his circumstances, he would have never, ever been able to give his brothers the mercy that he gave them. Not once did Joseph complain; instead, he continued to trust in God from situation to situation, the good as well as the bad. Joseph maintained an unexplainable level of peace in the midst of his trials that can only come from being close to God. He always knew that he was right where God wanted him and that God was always with him no matter what was going on. He never held a grudge against his brothers, never intended any harm to them, continued to provide for them and their families, and he forgave them willingly and completely. He wasn't in denial about what they did to him as some of us can be when others do wrong to us. Neither did he excuse what they had done. He blatantly told them that malicious intent was behind what they did to him. As a matter of fact, when they sent the bogus message to him that was supposed to look as though it was from their father, Joseph wept. Even though he had told them when they initially came to Egypt, I always felt that Joseph cried because he hadn't fully conveyed his forgiveness to his brothers to the point that they fully understood his forgiveness and were at peace with him in their hearts. First, when you forgive someone, it says that you are at peace with the person and his or her transgression against you. Secondly, you extend that peace to the person causing the transgression allowing them to be at peace with you. You see, what we must understand is that when you see the sovereignty of God in your trials, you have a peace about you that even you can't explain. You don't whine or complain. And, you're eager to obey all that God asks you to do in every situation whether you understand or not simply because you know that God has a plan and is in control. Also, you are willing to serve others, even those who wrong you. Another fruit produced by seeing God's sovereignty and responding to it is confidence. We have confidence, not in ourselves, but in the power of God.

> ¹³"Go, find out where he is," the king ordered, "so I can send men and capture him." The report came back: "He is in Dothan." ¹⁴Then he sent horses and chariots and a strong force there. They went by night and surrounded the city. ¹⁵When the servant of the man of God got up and went out early the next morning, an army with horses and chariots had surrounded the city. "Oh, my lord, what shall we do?" the servant asked. ¹⁶"Don't be afraid," the prophet answered. "Those who are with us are more than those who are with them." ¹⁷And Elisha prayed, "O LORD, open his eyes so he may see." Then the LORD opened the servant's eyes, and he looked and saw the hills full of horses and chariots of fire all around Elisha. ¹⁸As the enemy came down toward him, Elisha prayed to the LORD, "Strike these people with blindness." So he struck them with blindness, as Elisha had asked.
>
> (II Kings 6:13-18)

Elisha, the man of God, kept spoiling the battle plans of the king of Aram by constantly revealing his location to the king of Israel. Well, quite naturally, this angered the king of Aram just enough that he felt like he needed to deal with Elisha. So, he sent his officers to find out where Elisha was. Once his officers found him, he sent his army to surround the city where Elisha was. When Elisha's servant saw the army, he was shocked and didn't know what to do (v15). Many of us respond like this when we face trials and tribulations. Does "oh woe is me" or "what am I going to do" sum up your disposition when you're facing trials? Elisha's response was full of confidence because his eyes were open to the sovereignty of God and the servant's wasn't. I can only imagine what the servant was thinking of when Elisha told him that there are more with us than there are with them. Aw, to see the look on his face would have been…priceless. Our eyes need to be opened just as the eyes of the servant were. On many occasions, we need the help of others to get there just as Elisha had to help his servant. Elisha consulted with God and trusted Him to get them out of that predicament because that's where his confidence was to begin with; it never was in his own strength and abilities. Seeing God's sovereignty in the midst of trials gives us great confidence to face them and it keeps us free of worry and anxiety.

Comforting Others

Our experiences are not meant to be our own. We share with each other a multitude of things about ourselves, but many of us are very reluctant to share about the sufferings we have experienced, the things that we are shameful of or embarrassed by, whether we are responsible or not. These are the very things that God wants us to share. He doesn't allow us to experience sufferings out of futility, but for the benefit of others. That is after we have come to proper terms with what we've experienced. Let's take a look at II Corinthians 1:3-5 to see how God helps others through our very own sufferings.

> [3]Praise be to the God and Father of our Lord Jesus Christ, the Father of compassion and the God of all comfort, [4]who comforts us in all our troubles, so that we can comfort those in any trouble with the comfort we ourselves have received from God. [5]For just as the sufferings of Christ flow over into our lives, so also through Christ our comfort overflows.

Obviously, God does not want us to hide our painful experiences. Something important to remember is that when we hide our painful experiences, those experiences are the very things that we become so enslaved to. Concealed, those experiences will burden us. They will have a negative impact on how we feel about ourselves, other people, and the world we live in. By sharing our painful experiences with others, who are suffering, God works through this by comforting the suffering individual. Through this, He enables us to forge deeper bonds of friendship. Did you ever feel more at ease after someone told you that they experienced a similar tragedy as yours? Didn't you feel a little closer to them? As a matter of fact, some trials we face maybe for the sole purpose of sharing it with someone else (Luke 22:31). Suffering actually equips us more than we otherwise would have been to make an emotional connection with people who are going through similar experiences like ours. In reference to the above passage, here's how God works it all out. As God comforts us through all of the troubles we experience, we are able to comfort others with the comfort that we have received from God. Mind you, in order to be comforted by God, we must seek out the comfort that He provides. By our very nature, we tend to look for comfort in every place except for the place we should, or we look for a way out. The comfort we receive from God naturally equips us to comfort those in any kind of trouble. Notice that the Scripture says that we can comfort those in "any" kind of trouble. Our ability to relate is important, but not necessary. This is possible because it's not about our ability to comfort the suffering individual. It's actually about using the comfort that we've received from God and extending it to that individual. When you were in trouble, what did you do? Remember how passionately you prayed to God? Remember how you consulted His word and trusted that what He said is true? There's no difference when it comes to helping someone else. You must pull from that same source, the only source of true comfort, God the Father. As a young child, my dad kidnapped me from my mother and subjected me to physical and emotional abuse for approximately three years. Some of those experiences will remain etched in my mind until the day I die. He fought me like I was a grown man. For instance, I was slammed so hard into the wall by my head that a hole was left in the wall. This happened on two separate occasions, of which one was a Christmas morning. That's one Christmas present that I could have done without. It wasn't until days later when I stood with my back to the wall that I realized that I was lifted up off the floor when he threw me into the wall. I had to stand on my tiptoes to reach where my head had hit. Another time, he had me pinned down on the floor. While he straddled me, he had both of his hands wrapped around my throat and was literally choking me. As I gasped for air, I could have sworn that I was breathing my last breath. On another occasion, he came home intoxicated in the middle of the night. Without any regard that I had to go to school the next morning, he woke me up and physically kicked me in my butt outside the back door and told me to stay back there until he came out to get me. Then, he goes to sleep while I sit in the back yard. I stayed out there until about seven o'clock in the morning when he let me back inside to get ready for school. Some years ago, in an effort to make some sense of all this, I pondered as to why God would allow me to suffer through such cruel experiences. These experiences had left wounds embedded deep within my soul, scarring the very essence of my being. I knew without a shadow of a doubt that God loved me and that He was hurt by what I had suffered at the hands of my dad. After a few moments, my focus began to turn outwardly. I thought about the millions of other cases of child abuse that predated mine, exist today, and those that will happen long after I'm gone. I thought that God loves those individuals just as much as He loves me. God, also, knew that I would eventually come to follow His Son, Jesus. So, I concluded that He allowed me to experience that abuse as a means to equip me. I would be able to reach out to and make a connection with those that I may come across who have gone through the same thing. In other words, this could become my ministry. Besides, isn't that what God allowed Jesus to do for me? God allowed Jesus to suffer for my benefit – to bring me into a relationship with Him. So, in turn, I was allowed to do the same – to suffer in order to bring others to God. Although it wasn't quite the way I would have expected, I think God granted me a glimpse of this as a way of telling me that I was on the right path. Instead of dealing directly with people with an abusive background, it came via a friend of mine, whom I had shared this part of my life with and my ongoing struggles as an adult. He was raising two young boys of his own. While hanging out together for lunch, I began sharing some feelings that I recently dealt with days earlier as a result of my abusive past. After I finished, he commented that he was encouraged that he has the opportunity to hear what I'm going through because hearing about my experiences is helping him to become a more patient father to his two boys. This really solidified the decision I had made and helped me to get some real closure regarding those abusive experiences. Although, while in the midst of them, they can be pretty horrible, things like this have shown me that when we are able to help others through our bad life experiences, it turns them into positives. This counteracts the negative effect those experiences could have on our life from that point forward. Experiences like these can easily turn in to a situation where the individual turns to drugs, alcohol abuse, or suicide as a solution to his or her problems. These methods provide no assistance whatsoever in helping the individual deal with his or her issue, so that the individual may have a chance of reaching a viable resolution. In fact, it only damages the individual more, thus, making it even more difficult for them to attain any type of resolution from the dilemma that caused them grief to begin with.

Verse 5 of II Corinthians 1 says that the sufferings of Christ flow over into our lives. The first impression that I got from this Scripture is that when we make the decision to follow Christ, due to the dramatic change in our lifestyle, there are certain types of activities that are only associated with following Jesus that will bring suffering in our lives. Certainly, I had never experienced any type of ridicule or persecution from sharing my faith or suffered due to resisting the temptation to sin, prior to my conversion to following Jesus. These aspects simply weren't a part of my life. As my thoughts delved to a more profound level regarding what the Scripture meant, I believe that the following passage describes the meaning more accurately.

> [12]Dear friends, do not be surprised at the painful trial you are suffering, as though something strange were happening to you. [13]But rejoice that you participate in the sufferings of Christ, so that you may be overjoyed when his glory is revealed. [14]If you are insulted because of the name of Christ, you are blessed, for the Spirit of glory and of God rests on you. [15]If you suffer, it should not be as a murder or thief or any other kind of criminal, or even as a meddler. [16]However, if you suffer as a Christian, do not be ashamed, but praise God that you

> bear that name. ... ¹⁹So, then, those who suffer according to God's will should commit themselves to their faithful Creator and continue to do good.
>
> (I Peter 4:12-19)

Christ suffered undeservingly for something He did not do. He was completely innocent and was found without sin. As His followers, we should expect to suffer in the same manner, to suffer righteously, not for the wicked things we have done, but rather for the will of God (I Peter 3:17). As the Scripture says, don't be shocked as though something unusual was happening, but expect it all the more. As I stated earlier, Christianity and suffering go hand in hand and it should be considered a blessing to participate in the sufferings of Christ. Paul was firmly affixed on this desire (Philippians 3:10). Remember that some suffering, as a Christian, is a clear indication of one who has turned from a life characterized by sin and has chosen to live a life according to the will of God in a God-forsaken world. The rest of the world will not understand the things that you do living the life that you live for God. And we know what happens when people don't understand or come into contact with someone (or something) that is different than they are. They heap verbal abuse upon them, criticize, and flat out malign their very existence. Just look at what we did to Jesus, the Son of God. Yet, the example established by Jesus of enduring through such suffering is what we must hold steadfast to. We should fully commit ourselves over to God, who is faithful to perfection and persist in doing that which is good (v19). How well have you committed yourself to God through suffering and persisted in doing good? We can take heart in the fact that just as Christ's sufferings flow into our lives, for His sake, His comfort equally flows as well. Through our sufferings, God can use us to help people to come to know Christ, but we have to have an open heart and open our mouths and be willing to share those things we naturally tend to keep hidden.

Encourage Repentance

There's no doubt about it that we are all a bunch of sinners. No matter how different or better we think we are than others; we all are exactly the same when it comes down to it (Romans 3:9-20, 22b-23). We've all broken the Law of God, no matter which rule we've fallen short of (James 2:10-12). We have a tendency to compare ourselves to each other and quite naturally when we do, whom are we going to choose for comparison? Will it be someone better or worse than us? Of course, someone far worse than we are simply because we have this natural desire to want to look better than we truly are. Let's take a look at the message Jesus told His disciples from Luke 13:1-5.

> [1]Now there were some present at that time who told Jesus about the Galileans whose blood Pilate had mixed with their sacrifices. [2]Jesus answered, "Do you think that these Galileans were worse sinners than all the other Galileans because they suffered this way? [3]I tell you, no! But unless you repent, you too will all perish. [4]Or those eighteen who died when the tower in Siloam fell on them – do you think they were more guilty than all the others living in Jerusalem? [5]I tell you, no! But unless you repent, you too will all perish."

The extent to which we suffer is not an indication of our sinfulness, which is a concept that people in Jesus' day thought was true. He warned them that if they didn't repent, they would perish, also. It doesn't matter who you are. We all are under the penalty of death due to our own personal sin and will face judgment (Hebrews 9:27). Look around you! People die by the multitude day in and day out unaware of the fact that this is the last day of their life. That's something we don't think about, but it is factual. Jesus is trying to awaken us to our spiritual condition so that we can see our need and turn to Him; otherwise, we shall face the consequences that the unrepentant will meet someday. On a much smaller scale, I believe the suffering we see in this world serves as a constant reminder of what we have to look forward to if we remain unrepentant and pass from this world without Christ. We, also, see the frailty of human life and that we're all in the same boat. Being that life-threatening events can happen to anyone of us and at any time, it's a pretty safe bet that most of us will relinquish our lives unexpectedly. On the contrary, many feel as though they have time to "get right with God" as though they were born with an expiration date stamped on their foreheads. I have yet to come across someone with that information readily available. Only God knows that information (Psalm 139:16). The apostle James describes a man in reference to his life as a mist that appears for a little while, then vanishes. Our time is short and no one knows when his or her time is up. I've heard people say that so-and-so's time came too soon. Personally, I don't think there's such a thing as someone's number coming up too soon. Our days are numbered. The time to repent and turn to Christ is now!

Character Manifestation & Strengthening

In many ways, suffering is for our personal benefit. Although it may never become evident to us in this lifetime why we faced a particular ordeal, this is something that we must come to accept. The reason being, if for no other reason at all, is simply because it's in the Bible. And, not to blow your mind, but we are encouraged to consider it joy when we face these trials. So, how are we supposed to do that?

> [2]Consider it pure joy, my brothers, whenever you face trials of many kinds, [3]because you know that the testing of your faith develops perseverance. [4]Perseverance must finish its work so that you may be mature and complete, not lacking anything.
>
> (James 1:2-4)

This is not without a significant purpose in mind. That's what's so good about God is that we can trust Him with absolute confidence even when we do not understand any of the events that are taking place. We know that He has a purpose in it all that's for our benefit (Romans 8:28). This reveals an aspect of God's love that is so unfamiliar to us. I want to share a brief example from our produce industry to kind of help make this aspect of God's love even more apparent.

When harvesting tomatoes, there are five stages of ripening that are of concern for the harvesters. The stages in order are immature, mature green, breaker, pink, and red. The majority of the tomatoes that hit our commercial market are picked off of the vine at the mature green stage. This is because the tomatoes picked at this stage are able to tolerate the rough handling of shipping and hold the longest in storage, shipping, and on the supermarket shelves than tomatoes harvested during the riper stages. In order to get these tomatoes to the proper ripening stage and ready for the commercial market, they are ripened artificially in special temperature-controlled rooms where they are gassed with ethylene. This quicker, artificial ripening process does not come without a price. The consumers have heavily criticized tomatoes that undergo this process as having a subpar flavor. Tomatoes that have been fully vine-ripened (brought to maturity according to God's original design) are factually known to be far better tasting than their artificially ripened counterparts.[2] It is evident that the tomatoes ripened with the use of human intervention falls short in the end. Now, think about these questions for a minute. How do you feel when someone has sold you short of something you deserve? How do you feel when you're not quite prepared for a situation (an exam, interview, etc.) that you should have been better prepared for? Despite who's at fault, wouldn't you feel hurt, short-changed, wronged, or maybe you'd struggle with something much deeper like feelings of incompetence or low self-esteem? Only you and God know how you would feel. What I really want you to understand is that God loves you so much that He would never, ever do this to you. God loves you so much that He would never short-change you like this. He would do whatever it takes to make sure that you are the best you can be, complete and not lacking anything, even if that means you will have to endure hardship. Referring back to the

Scripture in James, it says that the testing of our faith develops perseverance. Well, what's the implication behind the phrase *testing of our faith*? It means that your faith is going to be pushed to your limits and beyond. It's like gold being refined by fire – it's heated up far above normal temperatures (I Peter 1:7). This is necessary because it's not considered persevering until you've exceeded your human boundaries – it's when you feel that you can't go on any longer. Perseverance is a sign of strength, not having to do with one's physique, but of character, which is of far greater value in God's eyes. The only way to accomplish this is to endure and suffer through hardships, which is what God uses to change and strengthen our character. Unfortunately, we oppose this, but God does not leave us alone to face these trials without His guidance. The same result that's in James 1:4 is reiterated again in II Timothy 3:16-17. God wants us to be thoroughly equipped, and we see that God has given us His Word to help us achieve this goal. We must allow ourselves to be taught, corrected, and trained by God's word. We must make a conscious decision that we are going to do it God's way no matter how hurtful or tempting it is to veer off and go about it on our own. Just think back to what we've learned from the harvesting of tomatoes when they are allowed to reach maturity the way God intended them to, they have the absolute best flavor that they can have, keeping in mind that consumers were more satisfied with the results. Now, when man decides that God's way just isn't good enough or is taking too long, he intervenes. The results end up being nothing short of a big fiasco. The tomatoes reach maturity by some far less sufficient alternative method, which produces a result that nobody is satisfied with. The same holds true to our approach to trials and tribulations that we face in our lives. When we commit ourselves to do it God's way and waiting on God, we reach that level of maturity, the completeness that James was writing about through the Spirit.

Remember what we talked about earlier that Jesus profited from persevering through suffering (Hebrews 5:8). We learn to persevere and more importantly, we learn to trust in God, which ultimately deepens and proves our faith in Him to be genuine. Approaching trials from this perspective, we will never come up short. But, if we decide to handle our challenging situations according to our own knowledge and abilities or if we bail out in the middle of the process, we may receive only a partial benefit or lose out on the prize altogether (Proverbs 3:5-6). Remember, it was Jesus who learned obedience through suffering. So, where's the joy in all of this? It's being a part of the high calling that God wants to share with us – His holiness!

Another personal benefit to suffering in our lives was echoed in the previous paragraph. The benefit that I'm referring to is simply learning to trust in and rely upon God. For those who are disciples of Jesus, I can't begin to stress how important this is for us to learn and put into practice. It is so contradictory to our nature that we should be extremely passionate about grasping hold of and incorporating this foreign concept of trusting in God into our daily lives. I often see this very dilemma in my own life as I strive to serve my Master. As I type this, reflecting back on my walk with God, I am reminded of times when I have been oblivious to my lack of trust in God and saw in hindsight how I hadn't trusted in God through a circumstance. Also, there are times when I just struggled through a situation wondering whether or not I was even trusting in God. As I think about Jesus and how He trusted God absolutely, He can sometimes be hard to relate to in some instances. Despite the fact that Jesus is the standard given to mankind by God and He is what I aspire to be like, I feel this way at times because along with His humanity, Jesus was fully divine. At best, I am a mere human being riddled with sin. This, of course, isn't a bad thing by any stretch of the imagination, but it does provoke me to peruse through the Scriptures for an example that I can relate to more. That's why God put examples of the lives of all these other people in His word so that we can draw spiritually from them too. In this case, I will look at an example from the life of Paul, the apostle.

> [7]To keep me from becoming conceited because of these surpassingly great revelations, there was given me a thorn in my flesh, a messenger of Satan, to torment me. [8]Three times I pleaded with the Lord to take it away from me. [9]But he said to me, "My grace is sufficient for you, for my power is made perfect in weakness." Therefore I will boast all the more gladly about my weaknesses, so that Christ's power may rest on me. [10]That is why, for Christ's sake, I delight in weaknesses, in insults, in hardships, in persecutions, in difficulties. For when I am weak, then I am strong.
>
> (II Corinthians 12:7-10)

This is a very powerful statement made by Paul regarding human pain and suffering. Paul understood the whole reason behind this "thorn" that had been placed in his flesh. It was there to keep him from becoming proud because of all of the things God had revealed through him. Just imagine all of the miraculous things that Paul had come to know and see over the course of his life in servitude to the Lord. To name a few, he had the miraculous gift of the Holy Spirit, had seen many revelations, was an apostle that was uniquely born and is responsible for writing most of the books in the New Testament. After all of this, what man wouldn't begin to think that this was from the works of his hands? Of course, these were the works of God. Paul pleaded with God to remove this thorn three times, but God refused. If things always went well for us or when we experienced a significant amount of success, we would quickly forget about God. We become very proud and don't rely on Him. In our own minds, we become self-sufficient and begin to rely upon our own abilities, which eventually leads to our downfall (Proverbs 18:12). So, essentially, what God had given Paul was a little gift, a reminder that his greatest asset was his weaknesses because this is what kept him dependent on God. This was accomplished through suffering, his "thorn." Suffering is what keeps us humble before God because it is one way that can open us up to seeing our weaknesses. Through suffering, we come to realize that we don't have control over anything that goes on in our lives. We only have control over how we decide to respond to those things. Look at what Paul did. He went to God to have this thorn removed; he knew he couldn't do it himself. Then, God pointed Paul to what was most important, His grace. That's what it's all about…the grace of God! Once Paul grasped this, he not only changed his perspective but gladly boasted in his weaknesses because he knew that the power of God was right there with him. It's not about what we can do, but about what God can do through us in spite of our deficiencies. Then, God gets the glory! Amen. From Paul's example comes a great indicator of whether or not we are relying on and trusting in the grace of God. We may not come to the point that Paul did, but have you accepted your weaknesses? Have you truly come to terms with the fact that you are human and have weaknesses? Or, instead, do you excuse them away, pretend they aren't there or do you feel that you are completely adequate and self-sufficient? In spite of your weaknesses or sufferings, do you continue to press on knowing that God is going to guide and bring you through? Or, do you persist in complaining, discouragement, and come to a grinding halt? If you identify more with the former instead of the latter of the series of questions, there's a good possibility that you are trusting in God, but don't get too ecstatic; this is not easily maintained, just as it isn't easily attained.

In the summer of 2006 began a long journey that would provide me a valuable lesson in trusting in God. In early June, my then wife and I separated due to some long on-going character issues present within each of us. The request for a divorce, by yours truly, is what prompted the separation. I knew full well that I didn't have a biblical reason for a divorce, but my heart had just gotten so hard to the point where I deliberately chose to disobey God. I just wanted out of all the unnecessary garbage that was going on. Thanks to one of the elders in my church that I called that night to inform of my decision. After I told him the decision I had made, he, first, held me accountable to the word of God, which I didn't expect anything different from someone who is a true follower of Jesus. Next, he genuinely listened to me, something that hadn't been done at all up until that point. Because of those two things, I am forever grateful to him. Deep down inside, I really didn't want to make the same mistake twice, and this time around, I had the knowledge of God branded on my conscience. A couple of days later, prior to Sunday service, the church elders, lead evangelist, my wife, and I met to discuss the matter at hand where it was reiterated that there wasn't a biblical reason for a divorce. After some discussion, it was decided that what would be best is to separate temporarily, work on our own character issues, then come back together again. I must admit that I walked out of that meeting thinking that it's going to be a long time before I make any effort to get back with her.

During the first three months of the separation, I was overwhelmed with anxiety because I had decided to continue attending the same church, and it would be obvious that something was wrong because my wife and I weren't sitting together. She was widely liked throughout the church. I dealt with an abundance of anxiety and fear because of my preconceived thoughts. I felt that everyone knew what was going on, and they'd all place the blame on me. Judging by some previous events, that wasn't such a far-fetched idea. In spite of this, I was very much convinced about the fact that I was going there before she and I ever laid eyes on each other, and there was nothing that was going to deter me from continuing. It was during this initial time alone that was probably the most beneficial for me. I spent a lot of time praying to God. I, also, studied and wrestled with God's word more intensely than I had before. Although still hardened, His word still impacted my heart even though I didn't initially see it. Studying the Scriptures helped me to see where my faith had gone. I saw that my faith had been proven to be lacking genuineness because it hit rock bottom when the testing of the fire came (I Peter 1:6-7). Initially, this produced more guilty feelings in me, and I just felt like I was being beaten up because all I could see in Scripture was the wrong I had done. But, I later realized that it was I, who was beating myself up and the Scriptures were actually healing my heart because I went in there seeking council and looking to get back on track, otherwise known as repentance. I memorized lots of Scriptures. Some I memorized like Psalm 103, which is one of my favorite Psalms, to help remind me of the hope that I had in God, and others I memorized like Titus 2:11-14 to help change my heart back to doing what God called me to do. A particular sermon preached one Sunday by our then lead evangelist from Matthew 27:11-56 reminded me of how much Jesus suffered for me so that I could escape the suffering that was rightfully due to me in eternity. It seems kind of odd that we'd forget something as important as that, but quite often we do. That reinforced the reason behind Jesus' command to us in regard to taking communion. We need a designated time to remember what He did for us. Most often, situations arise in our daily lives where our actions give no indication that we're even thinking about Christ hanging on that cross for us. When the preacher went to the passage and began reading for his sermon, I began reading silently along with him. As I read, I believe I tuned everything else out because when I walked out of service, I didn't recall him finishing the reading of that passage nor do I remember anything he said afterward. What I do remember as I read that passage for myself was that all I saw were scenes from the Passion of the Christ. I had realized that I had suffered over the course of my marriage nowhere near what Jesus did while facing His trials while here on Earth. I even thought about Him being so stressed, praying in the Garden of Gethsemane about what He was about to face that He was sweating drops of blood. This helped me to feel that I can do this and acknowledge that I've been through much worse than this in my life and I survived. If I can survive that and Jesus can suffer through what He did for me, then certainly I can endure through this. If I still had any desire left in me to file for a divorce, I believe, at that moment, it had been completely abolished from my heart.

    Another thing that helped me during this time was learning from my past. I took the time to reflect on the circumstances surrounding the mistakes of my first marriage. Initially, it took me a while to be able to do this. I think that I had so many things going on in my mind from the current situation that I wasn't ready to go there just yet. I blatantly didn't want to acknowledge the lessons that I knew were there for me to draw from. Eventually, over time, I began to acknowledge and embrace those lessons as to not repeat the same erroneous behavior. I'm grateful for that because a person's past behavior is a good indication of how they're going to respond in the future when in similar situations. Many people miss this concept and keep wondering why they find themselves in the same crazy, messed up situations over and over again. Instead of acknowledging and dealing with their contribution to what went wrong, they adopt the excused mindset which says that everybody else is at fault and I had nothing to do with what went wrong. If we fail to deal with our own behavioral issues, we are destined to repeat those same behavioral issues over and over again.

Finally, being able to talk to my closest friends helped me out a great deal. I am forever grateful to those who gave me a listening ear during this time in my life. Having the conviction to realize that I needed to talk to someone to get this burden off of my chest and taking the initiative to make it happen made a world of difference for me. I didn't have to carry this on my own neither did I want to. I was able to be real with what I was feeling without worrying about being judged. These weren't guys that were here to listen to me complain, butter me up and tell me, "There, there, everything's gonna be alright." They didn't just tell me what I wanted to hear; that does a person no good at all. I didn't want that. They encouraged me and were there for me, but I also knew that I could count on them to tell me what I needed to hear. I called that group of men My Confidants. Over time, far beyond the initial three to six months of the separation, I received a lot of encouragement from various people who knew what was going on. My friends made a difference for me, and for that, I thank God.

Early in December of 2006, far sooner than I had planned, I approached my wife. What motivated me to approach her was that, out of the clear blue, after having no contact since the meeting we had Sunday morning back in June, I received an email from her the Monday after Thanksgiving requesting prayers because her cousin had passed away the week before. Then, the following Monday, I received another email from her requesting prayers because she, due to no fault of her own, had lost her job. I remember that Wednesday, I sat at work wondering how she must be feeling having to deal with all of this. Her cousin passes away, she loses her job, and in a way, she lost me. Despite still feeling hurt, angry, and all of the other emotions I felt, I began thinking about her more while in the process forgetting about how I was feeling. I knew that I had to go to her no matter the outcome. I decided that the upcoming Sunday, which was December 10th, I would talk to her. I noticed that since our separation, she would leave service just before the end. The Sunday at service, I kept watching waiting for her to get up and leave. When she left, I waited until she got into the parking lot a bit where we could have some sort of privacy. Then, I went and spoke to her. We spoke briefly there in the parking lot, cracked a few jokes, and laughed a bit. From that point, we began to visit each other as we were still living separately; we ate out together and even began to sit back together at church after a little while. This seemingly fairy tale reconciliation only lasted for a couple of months. In February, another fiasco broke out, which for me became the last straw. There wasn't any contact between the two of us from that point on. We were separated for sixteen months prior to her filing for a divorce. During that time, I had grown immensely closer to God. Because of this, when it all was said and done, I found myself praying to God, thanking Him for my recent trials. I consulted with church leaders and close friends for advice and received words of encouragement and comfort as needed. With those who were in there helping me, I had been as real as I possibly could with what I really felt; I held nothing back. I really didn't want to continue being married to her. Despite my personal feelings, I knew that I had no choice in the matter. If she wanted to continue to work on the marriage, I chose to because I was surrendered to God. If I truly considered myself His follower, then He had already made that decision for me. I couldn't file for divorce from my estranged wife; so I had to patiently wait for her to come around or file for a divorce. Surprisingly, I was overall content with the situation, although there were quite a few moments of frustration.

My most frustrating moment throughout all of this arrived in the late summer of 2007, a couple of months or so before the divorce was filed. I woke up one morning and I guess the year and how many ever months it was at that point of not being able to move on with my life had taken its toll on me. I got up as I normally do, got dressed, and went off to work. I did this despite the strong feeling I had of just wanting to hide out in my house all day and be alone. I figured being at work might serve as a distraction to how I was feeling, which would turn out to be a good thing. When I got to work, I began to feel more and more miserable as the morning progressed. I realized that going to work was a mistake and I should have kept my behind at home. As I thought about why I was feeling the way I did, I began to realize that I was having a major struggle because I felt like God was just beating me to death. In my mind, I knew this was not true at all. The fact that I was dealing with another wretched, sinful human being is what the problem was. It wasn't from God. No matter how much I thought about the Scriptures demonstrating God's love for me, my feelings just wouldn't get in line with what I knew intellectually to be true. I needed some help because it became obvious that I wasn't going to defeat this on my own. It was going to drive me crazy before the day was over. Being that I was already misty-eyed and needed some privacy, I left my desk and went into a conference room. I called one of my confidants and pretty much spilled everything I was thinking and feeling on him. My feelings were so strong that my eyes welled up with tears and I began to cry. My friend helped me a great deal that day. It's not that he told me these deep, profound things or anything that I wasn't already thinking. He listened to me, pointed me back to Scripture, reassured me, and gave me an outside perspective, which is what I probably needed the most. After the conversation, I was able to gather myself and I eventually felt better, although I still wished I would have stayed at home.

Approximately two months after the February separation, I began meeting with a couple of church leaders to bring the situation before God's word in preparation for a possible divorce. As applied to my specific situation, we studied out the possibility of remarriage for me because that's the underlying question that you have when facing a divorce. Although God hates it, He has laid out some specific guidelines regarding divorce and remarriage for His people. You definitely want to have your convictions down pat ahead of time in a situation like that. When things explode is not the time to be figuring out what the godly thing to do is. Some of my friends were highly upset and angrier than I was about the whole situation. She seemed to be getting away with murder. She was still being carried on my insurance and was gladly using it; although I had plans to end that when my company's next benefits open enrollment came around. She had no accountability to me whatsoever, doing whatever she pleased, and it could have stayed like that for five, ten, who knows for how many years. Although the possibility of being in this situation for an extended period of time was by no means music to my ears, I can say from the bottom of my heart that

I was unexplainably at peace with the circumstances. Did I want out of the situation? Yes, but I was still experiencing peace. Did I like the situation? No, but I was still experiencing peace. I believe the peace that I had throughout the situation was validated when some that I attend church with told me that they couldn't tell anything was wrong by the way I carried myself. If I hadn't told them what was going on at the time, they would have never known. I had heard some ungodly advice about what I should do from some of my disgruntled friends about filing a divorce, but I responded that I didn't have a biblical reason for filing a divorce, and I was going to obey God. It was even playfully suggested that I should leave the church and God so to speak, file divorce, and then come back. This was absolutely not an option. Try and understand this. The focus of my attention was the fact that Jesus died for me. He endured an immense amount of suffering for me and He did not have to do one bit of what He did. If I had focused on anything other than that, there wouldn't have been a reason for me to endure through what I did. I would not have done it. Heed these words if you get nothing else out of reading this. When you become a disciple or if you prefer, a Christian – they're the same thing (Acts 11:25-26) – you live according to the word of God. You apply it to your life and do it. There is absolutely no other way. Period! Jesus went to the cross for you, so you do the same for Him (Luke 14:25-27). You make His death on the cross personal. He died for no one else, but you. That's how you have to look at it. If you're running around claiming to be a Christian and you're not living according to God's word – being a disciple – here's some advice for you. Get your act together quickly! Many people claim to be following Jesus but aren't even reading His words let alone following them (John 12:47-48). Jesus makes it very clear that if you aren't abiding by His words, you don't belong to Him and are not a follower of His. This is the difference between someone who's just being religious and someone who's a true Christian – true Christians strive to obey God's word no matter what. In conclusion, while in the middle of the divorce process, filed in October of 2007 and finalized in April of 2008, I was praying to God on one occasion. I began to nurture feelings of guilt and self-pity thinking thoughts such as why did I have to be a part of *another* divorce, especially knowing how God felt about it. How come this couldn't have been some other sin – which really didn't matter anyway because sin is sin in God's eyes, and it all produces the same destructive outcome. Suddenly, I paused right in the middle of my prayer and remembered that I had just studied some attributes of God's character only a couple of months earlier. This one attribute of His came to mind – God's omniscience.

> [5]Great is our Lord and mighty in power; his understanding has no limit.
>
> (Psalm 147:5)

I realized and exclaimed to God, "Wait a minute, you knew this would happen! You knew!" God knew that this would happen long before my wife and I ever laid eyes on each other. He knew and He allowed it to happen. So, that changed my whole perspective of the situation along with my mood. Instead of beating myself up, it caused me to ponder and ask God why. As I continued in prayer, I realized that it would be a shame to have gone through all of that and not have learned something from it. Especially, when there is something that I can take and use to help someone else find God. That would especially please and glorify Him. So, that's what I had determined to do. It's amazing how changing our very own perspective can dramatically improve our attitude and approach to difficult situations. There were lessons that I learned to help me grow to become a better man of God and to help me make wiser decisions in my life. In persevering through and learning something from this situation that I can use, I have a victory. Now don't misunderstand what I'm saying here. The victory is not in the fact that my marriage ended. The victory is in the fact that I saw what was in God's word, applied it to my circumstances, and waited on Him no matter what the outcome would have been. You can never go wrong when you chose to do something God's way because God's way is perfect and His word is without flaws (Psalm 18:30).

From this time in my life, there are a couple of other noteworthy things to mention. I was conversing via email with a friend of mine who worked at a subsidiary of my company. It was the Monday after I approached my wife in the church parking lot. As I was typing the email, telling him about the encounter, Romans 5:10 came to mind along with this lesson. Despite how much we hurt, sinned, and grieved, God in the person of Jesus Christ, still came to us in our most dire time of need to heal, save, comfort, and instill hope in us. I felt that I had imitated that to some degree. I had displayed the heart of Christ. I was completely shocked and wondered if that was spiritual growth that I was seeing in myself. I immediately hopped on the phone to call a couple of my close spiritual confidants to share this revelation and get some sort of validation and perspective outside of my own. Additionally, during those initial months of the separation, I felt like I related to Jacob a little bit because, as I said earlier, I felt as though I was wrestling with God. I felt this way because of my studying out the Scriptures to deal with the struggle in my heart in regards to following what I was feeling versus surrendering to God's word, not because of the supernatural experience that Jacob had that caused him to earn the name Israel. Of course, God always wins, but our success is always determined by how we respond. We can either respond submissively or rebelliously. If you find yourself a little confused as to which one to choose, always chose submission. I realized that as disciples, we don't live up to our name as we should. As the Israel of the New Testament grace, we need to wrestle with God far more often than we do regarding the matters of our hearts. Just think about the type of God we have who would even allow us to think that we can even wrestle with Him (I Peter 5:6-7)! We have a God that deeply cares about each and every one of us, but we must first humble ourselves. This is done by praying consistently and studying out His word. We must let His word cut our hearts and being persistent about it until it does; otherwise, we're just relying upon ourselves and doing our own thing. Remember the example that Jesus left for us in the Garden of Gethsemane the night before He went to the cross. He prayed three times in order to get His heart to the point where He was ready to go to the cross. How much more should we pray in preparation for carrying out those commands of God that challenge our hearts?

Security, Hope, & Fulfillment

As a prerequisite to revealing where true hope lies, it is appropriate to expose the façade in the things that we put our confidence in. On that note, I have four words for you to contemplate that categorize the things the human heart yearns for. They are power, popularity, pleasure, and possessions. The many things we vie against one another for as people fall into one of the aforementioned categories. Like kittens fixated on a ball of yarn, we chase after money, sex, relationships, material possessions, and the like. We go after such things in an effort to quench our thirst for hope, our need for security, and to prove our self-worth. Once we reach a certain status quo, we begin to look down on others who we feel haven't quite lived up to our standard. We do this despite the fact that we may be feeling empty inside, yet, giving the appearance of having it all together. That's the façade. These things are simply insufficient when it comes to providing hope. They are temporal, meaningless, and if we're not careful, they can enslave us. Putting our hope and trust in worldly things can lead only to one outcome. From Luke 16:19-31, we see the eternal impact this can have on an individual. Lazarus was poor, afflicted with sores, and had to beg for food while the rich man had it made. From the human viewpoint, this can seem so unfair for one man to have to suffer while another gets to live in the lap of luxury day in and day out without the slightest concern for those who are less fortunate. Two things aren't taken in to account. First is that God made us all (Proverbs 22:2). He is sovereign and we all have equal status under Him. Second is the great leveler, which evens the playing field. No matter what material possessions you have or what you've accomplished in your life, death befalls us all. After this, what do you have left? You're left only with who you were as a person to stand before God to be judged. And, this would not be a good time to be caught on the wrong side of justice. God will make every injustice right, and He will comfort His people for eternity. Let's get something straight before we go any further. I'm not saying in any form or fashion that all rich people are eternally condemned. Absolutely not! Although the actions of the rich man may seem harmless, there is a problem that is not so easily visible. The rich man's underlying problem is revealed in the following parable told by Jesus.

> [13]Someone in the crowd said to him, "Teacher, tell my brother to divide the inheritance with me." [14]Jesus replied, "Man, who appointed me a judge or arbiter between you?" [15]Then he said to them, "Watch out! Be on your guard against all kinds of greed; a man's life does not consist in the abundance of his possessions." [16]And he told them this parable: "The ground of a certain rich man produced a good crop. [17]He thought to himself, 'What shall I do? I have no place to store my crops.' [18]"Then he said, 'This is what I'll do. I will tear down my barns and build bigger ones, and there I will store all my grain and my goods. [19]And I'll say to myself, "You have plenty of good things laid up for many years. Take life easy; eat, drink and be merry."' [20]"But God said to him, 'You fool! This very night your life will be demanded from you. Then who will get what you have prepared for yourself?' [21]"This is how it will be with anyone who stores up things for himself but is not rich toward God."
>
> (Luke 12:13-21)

Right off the bat, Jesus warns us and makes it clear that who you are has nothing to do with what you have or how much of something you have whether its material possessions, natural abilities, or the company you keep. He couldn't have been more accurate in describing our condition. We sincerely believe that what we have makes us a good person or gives us a license to do whatever we want. When, in actuality, pride, disrespect, and selfishness are their defining characteristics. These characteristics are not exclusive to only the rich and famous or the high in popularity. We all, to some degree, have this characteristic embedded deep within us. Not only are those who have much are deceived about their true nature, but those who don't have as much are just as deceived. Individuals who have less tend to be attracted to those who have much in an effort to acquire something or improve their own status. Now, Jesus further expounds His point with this parable about this rich man that may come across as though He's condemning wealth, but in and of itself, wealth is not evil. In Proverbs 10:22, it clearly tells us that wealth is a blessing from God, and it comes without any consequences. Wealth does not necessarily mean having a lot of money or material possessions. When you think about it, there are many people who are poor and are very happy. On the other hand, there are others who are filthy rich and are equally as unhappy as they are rich. Wealth simply means having a large amount of something good or beneficial to our well-being. The real issue behind the wealth that Jesus is addressing here is hoarding or stockpiling, which refers to collecting an excessive amount of something and keeping it hidden for your personal future use. It seems to be that the man in the parable was already rich at the time the ground was producing good crops, so he was not dependent upon this; nor was it this production from the ground that made him rich. As Jesus gave no indication of how long this portion of the ground profited the man, it could have been responsible for bringing him to his current economic state depending on how long it had produced its crops. No matter the details of the acquisition of his wealth; at this juncture, he was well off and still receiving blessings of wealth from God. What needs to be brought to light is what was characteristic of this rich man's attitude in the midst of his blessings. Quite frankly, he was filled with pride, which resulted in ingratitude and selfishness. The first thing of concern was that he thought that all he had was solely from the work of his own hands when, in reality, it was a blessing from God (Ecclesiastes 5:19-20). There's no doubt that this man is a hard worker. That becomes evident in the fact that he has reaped what the ground is capable of producing. He obviously had to till the ground, plant the seeds, and harvest the crops. In addition to that, he was more than willing to tear down his old barns to build bigger barns to hold his surplus of crops. What was not a result of his hands is that the ground was capable of producing and the amount at which it produced. No matter how hard he would have prepared the ground, no matter how many seeds he would have planted, if that ground wasn't capable of producing what it did, he would have gotten absolutely nothing. Also, the very fact that he was able to acquire the ground, however it got into his possession, was not all the works of his hands. Those are blessings from God. This is a result of the rich man's pride. It says that we don't need God and causes us to live as though we are independent of Him. This led him to be ungrateful to God for all that He's given him. He, not once, acknowledged or thanked God for His abundance of blessings. Because of this, the rich man was only able to have an inward focus, thinking more of himself, when he was faced with the *dilemma* of what to do with his surplus. He gave no consideration to the will of God; thus, his selfishness gave birth to hoarding and he was willing to do whatever it took to make sure he accomplished this goal, even if it meant doing excessive work. He was looking forward to taking the rest of his life easy and being happy because of what he had stored away. He placed his security, hope, and happiness in all of his possessions. Proverbs 18:11 sums up this type of mentality, it says, "The wealth of the rich is their fortified city; they imagine it an unscalable wall." As a city, in biblical times, could be deceived about how well they were protected from intruders because of the wall at its circumference, the same holds true for those who are wealthy. The danger is thinking that you have it made in the shade because of the multitude of your possessions. Possessions are only a means to an end. They are temporary and are known to depart far more quickly than they arrive (Proverbs 23:4-5). And, not to mention, the ultimate fate of everyone is to die. All of your possessions are left to whomever and your hard work to acquire those possessions doesn't mean squat…at least not to you (Ecclesiastes 6:1-2). I'm sure the person who acquires the possessions you leave behind will appreciate all the hard work you've invested while they indulge themselves in the fruit of your labor, hence, God's response in Luke 12:20. It's foolishness! I am completely baffled when I hear some people say that at least they'll be able to say when they die that they had such and such and did this and that. People! Do you even hear what you're saying? First of all, unless something has changed without my knowledge, you won't be saying much when you die. Secondly, having material possessions, wealth, and the like do not equate to peace in our lives. On the contrary, it is a great catalyst for stress, illness, worry, and wrongdoing either against or by you. These are ever-present, but they become more and more apparent in particular situations such as in an economy that has suffered and been crippled as this country has been over the last several years.

As 2008 came to a close, I read a series of articles describing the hijacking activities of Somali pirates raiding ships off the coast of Australia. On one occasion, after hijacking an oil-laden Saudi supertanker for about $3 million in ransom, their boat capsized in a storm shortly thereafter. Five of the eight pirates drowned with their share of the ransom money in their possession. Reportedly, the other three made it safely to shore after several hours of swimming. If not all, most of the ransom money was lost.[3] The fate of the pirates should be of no surprise. Proverbs 10:2 says, "Ill-gotten treasures are of no value, but righteousness delivers from death." This serves as an example of the value we put on having money and material possessions. Many people are willing to go to great lengths of indecency, barbarity, and corruption in order to acquire money and possessions. The acquisition of wealth by illegal means only leads to judgment. There's no peace in it whatsoever. Those who attain their wealth illegally are only fooling themselves. If you're robbing banks, dealing drugs, and the like, you might get away with it for a while, but eventually, you're going to get caught. Even worse, you might lose your life as a result of it. So, how can you enjoy your wealth when you are constantly on the run from the police? How can you enjoy it when you have to watch your back to keep those you're running around with from stealing it from you? Wealth is a gift from God. When He gives it, He gives it without adding any trouble to it (Proverbs 10:22). Just think about it for a minute. Those who have acquired their wealth via respectable means have peace. They can enjoy their wealth without having to worry about all of the nonsense that those who acquire wealth illegally have to worry about. So, what about people who want to live the high life and resort to illegal methods to do it? As Paul said, they need to learn the secret to being content in any and every situation (Philippians 4:10-13). It is the love of money that drives people to commit the many iniquitous acts we see in our society from the white-collar crimes to the organized crime rings (I Timothy 6:6-10).

Due to the downturn of the economy in 2008, people began to lose their minds, thus showing where their security was in. Now, don't get me wrong. I'm not at all saying that thousands of lost jobs aren't something we need to be concerned about and those who lost those jobs should act as though nothing is wrong. I was very grateful to know that my company was taking steps to avoid layoffs of any of its employees and desired to protect the reputation it had over the years of not ever having to do so. What alarms me though is when you hear stories; for instance, a Massachusetts woman took her life because her home is about to be foreclosed on and sold at an auction.[4] You can't sit there and tell me that something isn't wrong with that. She sent a note to the mortgage company stating that by the time they foreclosed on the home that day, she'd be dead. This woman, who took care of the bills, left behind a husband, who was unaware that they were even being foreclosed on, and a son. She felt that she was helping them to avoid foreclosure on their home by committing suicide, which would allow them to use the life insurance money to pay for the house. I couldn't even begin to imagine how her family felt, especially her husband. This behavior is not unique to just common everyday people. Billionaires were killing themselves for losing their fortunes, too. I think that wealthy people are more prone to struggle with the loss of material possessions than people in any other class. It's just not human nature to want to live on less than we are accustomed to. If anything, we always want more because we are greedy by nature and don't know the first thing about being content with what we have. For anyone who is wealthy that all of a sudden has to live a meager lifestyle, that's a major shock and adjustment. That is a much greater fall than someone who is a middle-class citizen. This was part of the problem for a German billionaire who was so devastated by the impact the financial crisis had on his companies that he decided to take his life by throwing himself in front of an oncoming train.[5] Why did these people resort to this type of behavior? They, on some level, had their hope and security in their material possessions. When that was threatened or taken away from them, they lost all hope and felt it futile to continue living. Stories like these are very sad and heart wrenching but should confirm that material possessions do not bring security and peace. They are more likely to bring us stress, if we allow them to, because we view them as something they were never meant to be, and we expect something from them they were never meant to give. They cause us stress because we worry about how to keep what we have already acquired, and we can be consumed with how we can acquire more. This is one heck of a vicious circle to be caught up in. So, why are we caught up in such a predicament like this in the first place? It's simple. Material possessions do not fill us up. This is why we continue to desire more and are adamant about acquiring them, even to the degree of wronging others. Dealing with this phenomenon appropriately calls for an understanding of a fact that I alluded to earlier. That fact is that we have a void within us that can only be filled up by God. We are trying to fill that void because we are incomplete and as long as we try to fill that void with everything except what belongs there, we will remain incomplete. The void is there because we were separated from Him in the very beginning when man fell out of the grace of God. Jesus closes out the parable confirming that this is what life will be like for those who aren't rich towards God. Without God, we are destined for leading a dead-end and meaningless life full of anxiety, worry, and stress. This sounds pretty self-destructive if you ask me. But what more should we expect? It's merely the consequences of the choices we've made. The solution lies in putting our hope and security in that which is meant to give hope and security. Jesus Christ came to give us life to the fullest (John 10:7-10). All that's required of us is to listen and follow like good sheep with their shepherd. Doing so is when we'll arrive at having the peace that we so desire. Jesus puts the concept we have about material possessions into the right perspective when He said

> [19]Do not store up for yourselves treasures on earth, where moth and rust destroy, and where thieves break in and steal. [20]But store up for yourselves treasures in heaven, where moth and rust do not destroy, and where thieves do not break in and steal. [21]For where your treasure is, there your heart will be also.
>
> (Matthew 6:19-21)

We are not to store up things that are impermanent, but that which is permanent. Quite naturally, the things we keep or strive for are the things that we treasure, which indicate that our hearts have been taken captive. If our heart is wrapped up in temporal things, once those things are gone, what happens to us? This is just another perspective on why people behave the way they do and resort to suicide in situations like this. So, what are some specific ways that we can show ourselves rich towards God? To answer this question, let's refer back to the rich man in Jesus' parable. In analyzing the characteristics of his attitude, we came to the conclusion that he was prideful, ungrateful, and selfish. So, I reckon that a good starting point to being rich towards God would be to strive for characteristics that are in contrast to the attitude of the rich man. Those characteristics would be humility, gratitude, and selflessness. Now, the next step is to figure out what these characteristics would look like so that they can be incorporated into our lives. Looking at this from the perspective of the rich man and his situation, how could he have displayed these characteristics? Out of the sincerity of his heart, the rich man could have acknowledged and thanked God for all of the blessings bestowed on him. He would be acknowledging the fact that all that he had came from God. Finally, venturing back to the first parable of the rich man and Lazarus, what if the rich man would have been gracious to the condition of Lazarus by giving him something to eat or meeting some of his other needs?

These are just a few qualities that are indicative of someone who is rich towards God.

The Adversary

Many people see all of the bad that's prevalent in the world and criticize God and His abilities without even giving consideration to the fact that there is an adversary working against the purposes of God (Ephesians 6:10-12). Contrary to God's use of suffering in our lives, the adversary poses absolutely no benefit to us whatsoever. As a matter of fact, he looks to devour us like a roaring lion (I Peter 5:8). He is known by many names but is mostly referred to in the Scriptures as Satan. The Hebrew origin of the word "Satan" means adversary or opposer. Fitting with his nature, he was the very first being to sin (rebel) against God and coerced a third of the holy angels to do so as well. So, Eve didn't stand a chance against him when he confronted her in the Garden. He continues to diligently rebel against or oppose any and everything having to do with God and the fulfillment of His purposes. Don't read anything into this other than what was said. Satan can neither thwart God's plans nor can he do anything without God's allowance. By now, your curiosity may have peaked causing you to wonder why God didn't just destroy Satan when he initially rebelled. To tell you the truth, I haven't the slightest idea as to why, and it's really not for me to question every little detail of why God does what He does. He is God, the Almighty God. But, I do know and rest assured in the fact that God has absolute control over everything and He knows exactly what He's doing. In the way that God operates, there seems to be a process about everything in which He brings His purposes to completion over the course of time at just the precise moment. God does not operate as we do. It's so difficult for us to understand and accept what He's doing on many occasions because to us, He seems to be doing nothing at all. This difference is what causes so much stress in our lives as we strive to relate to our God. Just take a look back at the situation in the Garden of Eden. When Adam and Eve fell, Jesus wasn't there the next day to bring salvation to all of mankind. It wasn't until thousands of years later when He arrived on the scene. If left up to us, Jesus would have undoubtedly been there by nightfall. We are beings consumed by the concept of instant gratification, and in the world we live in, that reigns supreme. We want things here and now with no ifs ands or buts about it. Should we expect anything different from beings that are governed by the boundaries of time? God is outside the boundaries of time, yet He expects us to wait on Him to bring His plans to completion. I believe that there is a lot to be learned from this aspect of God. So, how this applies to our previous question is simply this. Satan's future is solidified; he is destined for eternal damnation and there's absolutely nothing he can do about it. Now, just imagine how enraged and bitter he is at God. Therefore, all there is left for him to do is to wreak havoc in opposition to God. Unfortunately, that equation is inclusive of all of mankind. He knows how much God loves and delights in us. Satan has an arsenal of weapons and schemes that he uses to attack and confuse us. The approach Satan uses depends on where you are in your relationship with God. An individual can either be in the dark – lost, not saved, have no relationship with God – or in the light – found, saved, have a relationship with God (II Peter 2:9-10). Keep in mind that there aren't any gray areas, works in progress, which results in sayings like "I'm working on it", or it could be better when it comes to salvation. It's either you are or you're not, case closed. Responses like those have everything to do with you and your abilities and nothing at all to do with Jesus. Remember that no matter what you do, there's absolutely nothing you can do to earn your salvation. Paul talks about this very thing to the Galatians in chapter 3. Now, let's pull back some of the tall grass so that we can get a visual of this enemy that's lurking within. He doesn't want us to know that he exists or become acquainted with his schemes because this works to his advantage and gives him the cover that he needs. Quite naturally, if you believe that an enemy doesn't exist or continues to be a threat, you won't equip and prepare yourself for battle. And, if you are unaware of his tactics, you won't know how to defend yourself. So, if you're completely oblivious to his presence and capabilities, know that he's prowling around like a lion hiding under the cover of the tall grass on the plains of the Serengeti, ready to pounce on the weak and unsuspected.

> [3]And even if our gospel is veiled, it is veiled to those who are perishing. [4]The god of this age has blinded the minds of unbelievers, so that they cannot see the light of the gospel of the glory of Christ, who is the image of God.
>
> (II Corinthians 4:3-4)

For those living in the darkness, I believe that his primary goal is to keep them living in the darkness. The more he can do this, the easier it makes his job. He keeps them from receiving the light, which is the truth of God, their most dire need. Their hearts remain, as the Hebrew writer puts it, hardened by sin's deceitfulness. Individuals in this condition think that the lifestyle they're living in opposition to God is what's appropriate, that it brings them joy, and fulfills their every need. I don't believe that Satan necessarily attacks those who are living in the dark, at least not in the same way he does Christians. He oppresses his children and keeps them in a ball of confusion and turmoil under his authority. Coming to the knowledge of the truth would set them free and bring them peace. So, he does all he can to thwart that because he doesn't care about you and doesn't want anyone having what he can't have. He incorporates two methods to keep his children from receiving the truth of God. They are prevention (Matthew 13:19, Luke 8:12) and perversion (II Corinthians 11:13-15). At these, he works energetically and continuously in an effort to achieve his goal. This becomes painfully obvious as you observe the daily activities of our world in contrast to the holiness of God's word. His influence in this world is pretty powerful. Don't be foolish by underestimating him. He is a formidable foe, and we're no match for him on our own. This is demonstrated in the very fact that the whole world is blanketed by lies and misconceptions and is living in total ignorance. For example, the misconceptions he has the world living under regarding sex have seemingly spiraled to even more profound levels of filth in part due to the advent of the technological age we live in. The concept of sex as a marketing tool has turned probably God's greatest gift meant to be mutually shared between man and woman into something cheap and sleazy, to say the least. Just think about all of the scantily-clad women and the over-abundance of sex scenes plastered throughout movies, television programs, and billboards that we view on a daily basis. On top of that, add in the myriad of sexual innuendos, and you have the right ingredients for poisoning our thoughts on the subject. For example, as I was driving yesterday, I saw an advertisement on a billboard for VW convertibles that read "Go Topless". Things like this are everywhere you go and influence your thoughts. It makes it next to impossible to stay pure in your thinking. In movies and on television, explicit scenes are abruptly thrown into the pictures. In most cases, they don't even fit into the flow of what's going on. It comes off as more of a distraction. But, nevertheless, they are there all because someone has to have an explicit scene in the movie or an advertisement so that they can make a sell. This is normal behavior for the majority of the world's population, but this is in opposition to God's design.

By the way, these visual aids aren't helping men one iota. It's only fueling one of men's most prevalent character flaws and prevents us from moving our thinking out of the prehistoric age. Because we are extremely visual and can draw sexual gratification from our surroundings, men have just flat out lost all control. The majority of men can't even begin to admire a beautiful woman without imagining what she looks like without her garments on or wondering what she would be like in bed. We've become so imprisoned by our lustful thoughts regarding women that for most men, it's inconceivable to have a platonic relationship with a woman. The ultimate goal of the whole relationship is to go to bed with them. And, this whole idea is portrayed to be some uncontrollable, innate instinct. This is so untrue. The problem why most men think this way is because we've given in to that sin too much that it owns us. When you choose to sin and it becomes a part of your character, it progressively worsens (James 1:14-15). In this case, men have given in to lusting after women so much that we've connected seeing a beautiful woman with going to bed with her. In our minds, the two concepts seem to be one, but they are not. They are two separate things altogether. Pure admiration of or having a platonic relationship with women is incomprehensible because of the choices men make and their lack of self-control. Without the truth of God's word functioning in our lives, we have no concept of purity, its importance, and its impact on us and our relationships with members of the opposite sex. All men, to varying degrees, depending on the individual, possess a lack of respect for women. That's a fact of the fallen nature of men. The lie that having sex with as many women as possible is something that *men do* or *makes you more of a man* proves that women are nothing more than objects to men. Some are really taken captive by this. *Getting girls* is made out to be a sport, a challenge, and an expression of their manhood. They refer to themselves by monikers such as pimps and players. The focus of their lives is to get with as many women as possible. They senselessly boast and brag and make claims, sometimes empty, about how many women they've been with in order to look impressive or manlier in front of each other. And, to add to the senselessness, they degrade their companions with remarks in the reverse.

Contrary to what men may arrogantly think, Jesus dispels any ideas about the virtue of their lifestyles. When Jesus answers the Pharisees' question about the lawfulness of divorce, He makes it clear what God's intention is between man and woman. He said, "…that at the beginning the Creator made them male and female…So they are no longer two, but one. Therefore, what God has joined together, let man not separate. (Matthew 19:4-6)." Essentially, what Jesus was saying here is that the ratio between man and woman, woman and man is meant to be a one to one relationship. They are to be bonded together so tightly that they are viewed as a single unit and they are to be bonded together for life. Think about this. God made one man in the beginning and He made one woman for that one man. Adam didn't have a number of women that he could choose to *get with* whenever he so desired or got tired of his current honey. He understood that Eve was his partner and his friend for life. The very absence of another woman made this clear. Then, from Adam and Eve's union sprang the rest of mankind. What was instituted in the beginning was meant to be carried on to the end. One man, one woman for life! Under the influence of the Holy Spirit, Paul confirms this same fact, along with some additional information, to the Christians in Corinth. In I Corinthians 7:2, he says, "But since there is so much immorality, each man should have his own wife, and each woman her own husband." He didn't say girlfriends, mistresses, friends with fringe benefits, or whatever other colloquialisms you want to attach to it. He said his own wife, own husband. Period! Anything outside of that is considered immoral. The circumstances surrounding the sexual immorality the Christians were being converted out of in Corinth was abysmal. Unfortunately, I can't say that our society today is any better. The one and only solution Paul gave the Corinthians to resolve all of the sexual immorality was marriage. So, what does this say about sex? God designed it solely to be experienced by a *man* and a *woman* within the bond of marriage…to each other. It's the deepest level of physical intimacy that is meant to be shared by and enjoyed just between the couple. It's an act that further bonds them together as one, otherwise known as consummation. If one has been sexually immoral, even if it's between the two that will eventually get married, you have to ask yourself. What's left for the marriage to make it special? What's left that has only been shared by the joined couple? This, in effect, destroys the sanctity of marriage. The purity that should have been brought to the marriage, which the partner is entitled to, is no longer available.

So, for you macho men who think that getting with multiple women is a challenge and an expression of your manhood, consider this – this type of mentality really shows you to be just the opposite – that you're not much of a man at all. It's really more characteristic of an animal, hence, the term dog that women so affectionately coined for us long ago. Your chasing after multiple women isn't a challenge at all but is indicative of your weakness, insecurity, cowardice, and lack of commitment. If you're looking for a real challenge, one that's fit for a true man, then, let's see how you measure up to this when the opportunity arises. When you get married and the normal course of marriage takes its toll, that is when those times of complacency and staleness rears its ugly head. Can you consistently make your wife fall in love with you over and over and over again by showing her your undying love and endless commitment to her with the same passion, force, and energy you exerted that inspired her to marry you in the first place? If your wife can walk in a room full of women and know that there isn't another woman in the room loved more by her husband than she (of course, there's really no way to determine if it's true or not, but if she feels that way in her heart), then, you've stepped up to the challenge of being a man.

Women aren't without their own misconceptions about the subject either. They have the idea that sex is meant to be empowering. They primarily put this principle into practice in the workplace and in the marriage. In the workplace, it is evidenced by things like the regular display of too much cleavage and short skirts that reveal too much of the upper thighs. It is employed as a tactic for competing with men in the workplace to help them move up the corporate ladder. On the contrary, statistics have shown that women who dress more provocatively in the workplace tend to suffer more than they benefit. They are less likely to advance up the corporate ladder and command higher salaries than their more conservative dressing counterparts. They, also, are less likely to be hired by an employer due to the message they project.

And, in addition to the workplace setbacks, their reputation can begin to take a turn for the worse due to their choice of business attire.[6]

In the marriage is where I believe this idea causes the most damage. Granted, God did create us, men and women, to be sexual beings. I believe that in most cases women can go far longer without sexual contact than men. I believe the reason for that lies in how God designed the man and woman differently in regard to their sexuality. Now, let me translate what this idea means as applied to the marriage. It's really all about gaining control. It involves using sex as a weapon to manipulate the man into getting what you want.[7] For women, this use of sex as a weapon is about power just like rape for men is all about power. This is an extreme act of selfishness. With the large number of men out there who have been unfaithful to their wives, there are women who are doing this to husbands that are faithful. Those women who have been cheated on by their husbands would probably have a bone to pick with you. For those in this category, the next time you decide to play this game, ask yourself these questions. Are you grateful for your faithful husband? Do you appreciate his faithfulness? If you say yes, but are playing this wicked little sex game, then you're lying to yourself. You know, "...a faithful husband has no choice but to come to you for sex."[8]

God's intention for this is very different than what we've come to use it for. Let's revisit I Corinthians, chapter 7 again to see what His intention was from the beginning. We already found out through Paul as he addresses the Corinthians that there is a one-to-one ratio between men and women and sexual needs are to be fulfilled only in marriage. Well, immediately following that information, Paul reveals the expectations for the frequency of that physical intimacy.

> [3]The husband should fulfill his marital duty to his wife, and likewise the wife to her husband. [4]The wife's body does not belong to her alone but also to her husband. In the same way, the husband's body does not belong to him alone but also to his wife. [5]Do not deprive each

> other except by mutual consent and for a time, so that you may devote yourselves to prayer. Then come together again so that Satan will not tempt you because of your lack of self-control.
>
> (I Corinthians 7:3-5)

We see here that sexual fulfillment should not be withheld by either partner in a marriage. The only time it's permissible to refrain from sexual activity is by mutual consent and prayer. It was never meant to be used as a tool for manipulation or punishment. The standard set by God is that it is meant to be freely given to the point of quenching your partner's desire. When you enter into that union, you no longer have sole possession and control over your body anymore, but you share that 50/50 with your spouse. It's their right and your responsibility. If you can't abide by that, then the suggestion is that you shouldn't get married. As a matter of fact, one of the main problems with marital relationships (and dating relationships to a degree) is that we don't understand or accept this one concept, and we do all sorts of things to try to avoid it, but it is interwoven into what a relationship is all about. It's the concept of sharing. The fact is that in a relationship, you lose a part of your personal identity and have a legitimate responsibility towards your partner (Genesis 2:24). Remember, the two become one. What did you think that meant? Relationships are that way by God's design, and there's no way to avoid it. People get into a relationship and seriously expect to do everything they did when they were single without any regard or say so from their partner. Couples decide to move in and just live together to *try it out* and see if the relationship will work before going to the next level. But, what this is really saying is that at the first hint of something I don't like, I'm out of here. There's no commitment whatsoever! In fact, studies have shown that couples who cohabitated together prior to getting married are more likely to divorce.[9] You're starting off on the wrong foot before you even begin. Besides, have you ever thought about what just living together says about you or what kind of message that could be sending? Could it be reflective of your attitude towards relationships? Couples need to stop toying around with the minor technicalities of their relationships and get down to the heart of the matter. Are you going to be committed? If not, then I suggest you move on. Reverting back to our original topic, sexual fulfillment was created for three primary reasons, which are procreation (Genesis 1:27-28), enjoyment (Proverbs 5:15-19), and, as with all of His creation, to glorify God (Hebrews 13:4). Now, you may pose the question, "What if there's an argument, or he does something I don't like?" This is a big contributor to withholding sexual fulfillment. People try to punish their partner to get back at them. It's a doggone shame that when problems arise in the marriage, the first place the war begins is in between the sheets. I personally believe that there is absolutely no correlation between the two at all. When there is disharmony, what is the priority or main objective? In

Ephesians 4:26, we are told that we shouldn't let our anger outlast the day it occurred in. So, the main objective is to restore peace within the relationship as soon as possible. Thus, the beckoning for sexual fulfillment typically shouldn't even come into play since the main focus should be restoring the harmony that's been lost. It may be engaged in to consummate the reconciliation. That's why makeup sex, as it's called, is so good because it sort of consummates the relationship again – it brings the two of you back together again – makes it official. Both, sexual fulfillment and being at peace with one another, each come with a critical warning. They both explicitly warn against giving Satan an avenue inside. Disharmony and the lack of sexual fulfillment are easy ways that Satan can come in and wreak havoc on your marriage relationship, potentially bringing it to its demise. So, you will do well to pay attention to the warning and take heed. In most cases, this type of mentality reveals a lack of forgiveness due to the individual's own incompetence or a lack of resolution between the two parties.

Such misconceptions, or more appropriately lies, prevail in our world. What I am capable of discussing won't even cover the tip of the iceberg. The whole world is under a myriad of lies like this that influence every aspect of life and causes mass confusion. An attempt to discuss every one of them would require a massive set of encyclopedias. Some examples of this pertaining to spiritual matters are that Christ was not deity; salvation is something that you can earn, and you can get away with rebellion against God. In addressing one of the aforementioned, the deity of Christ, the Scriptures make it clear that our Savior was fully divine when He graced the Earth with His presence. To aid in understanding this, we must try to grasp things the way the Jews did when they heard it. I believe they had a much deeper conviction about who God is than we do now. You understand why I say that if you heard all of the crazy things that are said about God these days. The Jews knew that there are certain attributes that can only be attributed to God and to no one else such as He is the Creator of all things, His eternal nature, only He is to be worshiped, and His proper name(s). In the following passages, you will find these exact same attributes ascribed to Jesus Christ. See Colossians 1:15-17 to see Christ as the Creator. See Isaiah 9:6-7 to see the eternal nature of Christ. See Matthew 8:2 and Hebrews 1:6 to see Christ being worshiped. See Jeremiah 23:5-6 to see a proper name of God used in reference to Jesus Christ (Jehovah Tsidkenu). For more direct confirmation, in Hebrews 1:3, we see the passage explicitly says that Jesus is the exact representation of God's being.

For some examples that are more down to Earth, we can look at the divorce rate in this country to determine the lie being lived out. Although we divorce at an alarming and ever-increasing rate, especially in Hollywood where they seem to marry and divorce as a publicity stunt, divorce was never, ever, ever, a part of God's design (Malachi 2:16, Matthew 19:3-6). It is never commanded in Scripture, only given as an option in a couple of situations. Another lie we live according to is being independent, or we like to consider ourselves a self-made man (or woman). How is it that we can honestly think that we got to our position in life without any help from anyone else? The job I have or some of the things I've learned, those came with the assistance of someone else. To the very core, we are such prideful beings. We don't want anyone to have any say in what we have achieved, yet we claim to have taught someone everything they know. The Bible makes it clear that no one can achieve success without getting assistance (Proverbs 11:14). Another lie, one that really gets me is that we are our own truth. We decide the truth for ourselves. Are you serious? Isn't that what got us in this mess to begin with? There are so many kinks in that one; I wouldn't even know where to begin.

If people decided the truth for themselves were true, I think that we'd have no basis or grounds for bringing someone to justice or punishing them when they did wrong. Even more so, in our daily interactions with each other, we'd have no right to judge or say anything detrimental against what someone else said or did. In both circumstances, a person would simply be acting out of the truth in their own heart. This would give them a right to do so without any opposition from anyone else. But that's not the case. There are a few characteristics of the truth that need to be made note of. First, the truth doesn't change from situation to situation but stays the same across the board. It is not meant to be altered in order to fit our needs or give us an advantage. Second, there is no such thing as multiple truths, which is essentially what one is saying when they make the claim that people decide the truth for themselves. There is one and only one. Jesus said, "I am the way and the truth and the life. No one comes to the Father except through me." He said this to indicate that He was the only path that led to God. This is even indicated in our speech. Whenever we refer to the truth, it's always preceded by the definitive article "the", which indicates that only one exists. Third, the truth doesn't find its origin in that which is subject to it. Just as the law we abide by in society doesn't originate from the general population subjected to it (but, from specially elected officials called the legislative branch of the government who are subjected to it outside of their legislative positions), the same concept holds true for the truth. It comes from a higher source.

On those living in the light, Satan has engaged in an all-out, on-going war (Revelation 12:17). And, to go along with the war, he has an arsenal of weapons to fit the occasion too. In an effort to help familiarize and prepare you against this nemesis, here's a crash course in some of the weaponry he likes to use during his battle against us. If you follow Christ, it would be a good idea for you to take to the Scriptures to get to know this enemy of ours. As I mentioned earlier, this is to his advantage if you stay in the dark about who he is.

First, Satan loves to create doubt within us. Look at what he did with Eve in the Garden of Eden (Genesis 3). If he can get us to second guess about anything that God has said, especially about matters dealing with God's grace and salvation, then he has us right where he wants us. We must be students of God's word and fight Satan's lies with Scripture as Jesus did when Satan confronted Him in the desert (Matthew 4).

He also loves to hinder the services of the saints (I Thessalonians 2:18). He absolutely hates to see the work of God done. For me, this could have very well been why the basketball ministry had been such a pain in making each session come together on time during that first year, despite the fact that I put the process in motion far enough in advance that it should have been completed on time. This became so frustrating to me that at times I questioned whether this ministry was God's will or not. After studying out the character of Satan and seeing this attribute, I thought how absurd it was for me to even entertain the thought that this could possibly not be God's will. Of course, it was! God wants His Word and the gospel of His Son preached to the ends of the Earth. Satan wanted me to become discouraged enough that I'd quit hosting the league, and I have to admit, I became discouraged enough that at times I did think about it.

Another method he uses is the infiltration of the church (Matthew 13:24-30, 36-43). What better way to destroy your opponent than attacking them from the inside out. He does this via the heavy use of *false teachers* (II Peter 2:1-3). He incites them to teach *false doctrines* (I Timothy 1:3-4, 6:3-5), which is only good for instigating quarrels and controversy. Then, if not put in check, it can lead to *divisions* in the church (II Corinthians 2:5-11). Looking a little deeper into the II

Corinthians 2 passage, we see the subtlety that Satan can use in his deception. Here, a brother committed a sin which, in turn, caused the church to enforce some discipline. And, they were more than right in doing so. But, the discipline that was inflicted on the individual was far too extreme. It was so extreme that it was devoid of love and it exemplified a lack of forgiveness, which should never, ever be the case. This can lead to someone becoming overwhelmed by guilt and excessive sorrow. Satan can take the use of sound doctrine and push it to the extreme in order to turn it into something horrible. In this case, he took appropriately administered discipline and forced it to the degree that it excluded love.

Next, he loves to persecute the church (Revelation 2:10). When persecution comes in its many forms, people have a tendency to become faithless and discouraged. Many have fallen away on account of persecution (Matthew 13:5-6, 20-21). The two best remedies for battling persecution is being deeply rooted in the word of God (v21a) and as Paul tells the Corinthians from the example of the apostles, you endure it (I Corinthians 4:11-13).

He tempts us to sin. He is constantly at work and always looking for ways to tempt us to sin. He will do whatever he can and use any method he can to get us to stumble. Now, don't make the mistake of thinking that this is an excuse to get you off the hook. Saying "Satan made me do it" doesn't fly. He can't make you sin. He can only present situations to arouse your desire to sin. You're the one who actually makes the choice to do so (James 1:13-15). Remember, it is human nature to pass the buck, but being a true Christian means taking personal responsibility for your own faults. So, what are some ways he tempts us to sin?

He tempts us to trust in ourselves and our own abilities (Proverbs 3:5-6). Satan wants us to stop relying on God and to start thinking that we know what's best for our lives. If you need a reminder as to why this is not good for us, please refer back to Adam and Eve in the Garden of Eden (Proverbs 14:12).

He tempts us to lose our faith in God (Luke 22:31-32). Satan wants to separate us from God and he can easily accomplish this if he can destroy our faith in God. As a remedy for this malady, we are told to resist him by standing firm in the very thing that he is trying to destroy (I Peter 5:8-9). You can stand firm, and you aren't doing this alone. Knowing that you have a fellowship of believers who are enduring through the same things alongside you provides a great deal of strength and encouragement. When you resist, with the strength of God, Satan is sure to high-tail it out of there (James 4:7).

He tempts us to lie as he did Ananias and Sapphira (Acts 5:3). When we lie, it is simply another way in which we trust in our own abilities and resources. Satan is the father and source of all lies, so every time we lie, we have allowed him to use us for his purposes.

He tempts us to be immoral. As I discussed earlier, he's got the whole world steeped in lust and sexual immorality. Yet, that doesn't stop him from tempting us into giving in. It's blatantly displayed for all to see and hints of it are everywhere. It's in the media, on the billboards, in the workplace, and on the Internet. You just can't escape it. Wherever you go, there's some kind of sexual connotation or image messing with your senses.

He tempts us to be preoccupied with the ways of the world (I John 2:15-17, Matthew 13:7, 22). Satan wants you to get caught up in the behavior of the world because it is governed by the system that he instituted (I John 5:19). To become preoccupied with worldliness would mean that you have turned your back on God.

He tempts us to be proud. This was the problem that caused Satan to fall from heaven (Ezekiel 28:11-17, Isaiah 14:12-15). He became filled with arrogance and wickedness because of the beauty that God had given him. He was so engulfed by his own splendor that he believed that he should have the Most High position rather than God. He planned to make himself like God forgetting that it was God who was the source of his existence and all that he had. Correct me if I'm wrong, but doesn't this sound like a description of fallen man? Pride is a very dangerous thing. Some pieces of evidence of pride are not listening, thinking you know-it-all, haughtiness, or thinking you deserve something. It could even be said that it is the source of all sin. This is why we must strive with all of our might towards living lives of meekness and humility. Our first step towards humility is trying to keep a vivid picture of who God is. As majestic and awe-inspiring beings as angels are to men that to have one in your presence literally drops you to your knees. Remember that these are the same majestic and awe-inspiring beings who constantly sing the praises of God because His majesty greatly surpasses theirs (Psalm 89:5-8).

Finally, he tempts us to discouragement, so that we will lose hope and give up on our walk with God. But, we know that He who is in us is greater than he who is in the world. So, we have the reassurance of knowing that as long as there is a God, we know that there is always hope.

Wrath of God

The fate of mankind without Jesus Christ is destined to succumb to the wrath of God (John 3:36). I've always thought that the fate of mankind was analogous to a man waiting on death row. He may go about doing his deeds in the confines of his little world, with seemingly little or no regard about the consequences, but sooner or later, he's going to have to pay the piper. So, the inevitability of the outcome is not the question. The question is "How long is the wait going to be?"

Contrary to what many of us may think, God's wrath is not reserved for the end times. Let's take a look at a passage we touched on earlier.

> [18]The wrath of God is being revealed from heaven against all the godlessness and wickedness of men who suppress the truth by their wickedness, [19]since what may be known about God is plain to them, because God has made it plain to them. [20]For since the creation of the world God's invisible qualities – his eternal power and divine nature – have been clearly seen, being understood from what has been made, so that men are without excuse.
>
> (Romans 1:18-20)

In my opinion, this passage, starting in verse 18 continuing on through to the end of the chapter, is really the beginning of the gospel. This is why it's at the beginning of Romans, a book centered on the grace of God. In order to come to Christ, we have to be made aware of our need for Him. As Christians, in order to have a deep appreciation of what we have in Christ, we need to see what we had to look forward to without Him. This passage does just that for us by revealing mankind's predicament before a holy God along with a detailed explanation for such predicament. Unfortunately, that's not within the scope of our discussion, so we won't go into much detail about that. What I do want to discuss is what the passage says about when God's wrath would be administered. It says that God's wrath is being revealed. Did you catch that? For a quick refresher course in English, the verb "is being revealed" is in the present perfect progressive tense which designates that an action or event started in the past and continues into the present with the added sense that it is an on-going action or event. So, what's the implication here? It is the fact that God's wrath has been poured out on mankind ever since the fall of man. It is seen unleashed all throughout Scripture in response to man's wickedness. You've seen it against Sodom and Gomorrah, against the rebellion of Korah and his followers, against Ananias and Sapphira, and against Christ as He bore the sins of the world on the cross. This will continue to be true until the consummation and the full extent of His wrath is released at the end judgment. I know this may cause your curiosity to skyrocket and many questions to come to mind regarding this, but I'm going to address a little on this one question. Who? Who is God's wrath aimed at? The answer is embedded right in verse 18. It's targeted at the "godlessness and wickedness of men who suppress the truth by their wickedness." Now, there's something in that statement that I find particularly interesting – the usage of the word "suppress," even more so, the phrase it's within, "men who suppress the truth." The word "suppress" means to prevent something from being seen or expressed. The word as applied to the passage pertains to something from within. So, what could this possibly mean? It means that all men, by design (Genesis 1:27), possess, within them to some degree, the truth about God and the reality of His existence. Men know deep within that there is a Supreme Being. God would not create us without some kind of innate knowledge of who He is or where we came from. But, men neither allow this truth to be manifested in their lives nor do they seek to build upon this truth. Despite having this inner knowledge, which culminates in a need to worship Him, we, instead, have resorted to worshipping ourselves, images, and material things (v21-23). While I was finalizing the manuscript for this book, I took the Seven Habits of Highly Effective People training course. Throughout the entire course, as I listened to the concepts that were taught, I couldn't help but think about the Scriptures and principles from God's word that was seemingly the foundation for many of these concepts. I don't know if the concepts of this course were lifted directly from the Bible when it was put together, but what this confirms for me is that God's word is the supreme authority. Whether we choose to live by it or not, His word is the chief cornerstone from which life is built. When we decide not to live according to His word – separate from Him – our life begins to progressively crumble at the rate in which we indulge ourselves in those things that destroy (Luke 15:11-16). By now, you may be wondering what part suffering plays in all of this. Well, it comes as a result of being under the wrath of God, the consequence an individual suffers for their rebellion.

> [24]Therefore God gave them over in the sinful desires of their hearts to sexual impurity for the degrading of their bodies with one another. [25]They exchanged the truth of God for a lie, and worshiped and served created things rather than the Creator – who is forever praised. Amen. [26]Because of this, god gave them over to shameful lusts. Even their women exchanged natural relations for unnatural ones. [27]In the same way the men also abandoned natural relations with women and were inflamed with lust for one another. Men committed indecent acts with other men, and received in themselves the due penalty for their perversion. [28]Furthermore, since they did not think it worthwhile to retain the knowledge of God, he gave them over to a depraved mind, to do what ought not to be done. [29]They have become filled with every kind of wickedness, evil, greed and depravity. They are full of envy, murder, strife, deceit and malice. They are gossips, [30]slanderers, God-haters, insolent, arrogant and boastful; they invent ways of doing evil; they disobey their parents; [31]they are senseless, faithless, heartless, ruthless. [32]Although they know God's righteous decree that those who do such things deserve death, they not only continue to do these very things but also approve of those who practice them.
>
> (Romans 1:24-32)

At the beginning of verses 24, 26, and 28, it tells us exactly how God is currently administering His wrath. From an earlier discussion, I mentioned that God abandons men over to their wicked and depraved actions as an act of judgment. In case you're wondering why God would do this or how this is an act of judgment it's because God is allowing a person's sin to run its full course on his or her life. We know from earlier that sin is only good for one thing......that's destruction. So, since that individual decided to follow what is untrue, God allows that person to be consumed by the consequences of their own sinful acts. Have you ever wondered why you weren't experiencing the quality of life you once imagined? If so, it probably would be a good idea to evaluate your lifestyle and the choices you've made. In case you haven't heard or figured it out, the choices we make become our habits, our habits become our character, and our character becomes our destiny.

In this passage, we see three distinct ways in which God's wrath is displayed on the wicked.

First, it says they were given over to the sexual impurity for the degrading of their bodies (v24). In today's society, there are so many people sleeping around with each other, it's more like an all you can eat buffet. Because of all the sexual immorality, a person is subjecting themselves to potentially catching one of the many diseases transmitted through inappropriate sexual conduct. This is so dangerous because we are sexual beings by design. With any activity short of abstinence, people can easily be taken captive by this and lose control. This is why Paul urged marriage partners to fulfill each other's sexual desires. It's God's desire for married couples and it reduces your spouse's temptation to stray and meet the need elsewhere. This is by no means an excuse for unfaithfulness. Diseases can be spread so rapidly via sexual contact. These diseases, especially true of AIDS, can reduce the quality of your life or destroy you altogether.

Second, they're given over to shameful lusts – women inflamed for women and men likewise for men (v26-27). Homosexuals are facing their many trials because their sexual preference is something that's completely unnatural. They're even trying to force it into something that's natural by wanting to legalize gay marriages along with having the same rights as heterosexual marriages. They, also, want to have normal families and raise kids like everyone else, and they have a fit because they run into all kinds of opposition. Let's face the facts. It's not a natural thing for men to have sex with other men and women with other women or to become joined together as though they were man and wife. And, don't say that God made you that way because He didn't. This is a choice that you made because of your sin. When God said that there wasn't a suitable helper for Adam, what did God do to resolve the problem? God created and gave Adam a woman named Eve (Genesis 2:20-24), not a man named Eric. He did this because that is the way it is supposed to be.

Lastly, they are given over to a depraved mind to do things that simply shouldn't be done. From within the depth of their wicked minds, people will conjure up the vilest of things to do or say. The world is full of people practicing inappropriate behavior. These actions can be limited to violating only the individual committing the act or it can be violations against another person, a group of people, or even animals. In recent news, you can read about a man caught red-handed having sex with a horse that he was already on probation for having sex with from a previous occasion. In another story, a retired professional athlete is suddenly murdered by his deranged mistress. Immediately after, she commits suicide. Both of their bodies were found together. His wife and children had no idea he was having an affair. Yet another story about a man who was so consumed by his hatred and bitterness of women because he hadn't had a girlfriend, a date, or slept with a woman in years that he walked into a women's fitness class and opened fire. He killed three women and injured nine before he turned the gun on himself and committed suicide. These randomly selected stories are only a small sample of the wickedness we're capable of. You get up every day not knowing what you're going to run in to. You just never know what that person you're sitting next to on the bus or the person you're walking next to in the mall is experiencing in their lives and how they're going to respond to it.

These three categories that God gives people over to aren't just some randomly selected areas but have a significant outcome that emphatically reflects the destructive nature of sin. I believe that these three categories represent sin's destructive ability in destroying the existing people, their ability to reproduce, and their ability to live in harmony and peace with themselves, each other, and their surroundings. Just think about it for a moment. All of the immorality and sexual sins in today's society are destructive, not necessarily in just a physical sense, but they produce deep emotional wounds that some may never heal from. There are many women who will never be the same after experiencing rape or being preyed upon and manipulated by men for their own pleasure. Think of the deep emotional scars that little boys and girls suffer after being sexually molested. Next, there's homosexuality – need I say more? Despite the excruciating pain experienced in childbirth, women have this deep innate desire to bear and raise children. It's their God-given assignment. Remember the women of the Old Testament who stressed and felt incomplete because they were barren. They cried out to God as to why they were under such a great curse and wanted to be blessed with the ability to bear children. Therefore, for women to become so inflamed for each other is the epitome of a society overrun with the wickedness of homosexuality. When homosexuality reaches its extreme, reproduction ceases right along with the race's ability to continue its existence into the future. Lastly, you can look at the news and read the papers every day to see every bit of the attributes from Paul's list (v29) working its magic at keeping peace and harmony at a distance. The human race is innovative and on the leading edge when it comes to acts of wickedness. At the most extreme measure, these categories unite together to remove the existence of the human race altogether.

Freedom from God's wrath, the present and the wrath to come can only come through Jesus Christ (Romans 8:1-4). Because of our sins, we are bringing on ourselves and others as well a lot of suffering in this lifetime with only an eternity of suffering to look forward to. Through Jesus Christ, we are set free and have the power to resist the temptation to sin (Romans 6:11-14).

CHAPTER THREE

Is God Doing Anything About It?

Many people question and criticize whether God is doing anything at all about the suffering in the world. People often ask these types of questions because they have their own ideas about dealing with the issue. Typically, it involves nothing short of getting rid of pain and suffering altogether. But God, let me tell you, has gone far above and beyond our expectations when it comes to resolving the issue of pain and suffering in the world. For those who profess to be Christians and are confused by the issue and are asking these very types of questions, I'd have to bring your Christianity in to question. This, of course, is not to offend you, but how could one proclaim to be something without having a basic understanding of the foundation that brought the very thing into existence? This statement, I hope, would motivate you to dig deeper into finding answers from the Scriptures. The gospel is a covert operation by God to rescue all of mankind from the eternal consequences of sin. Although the signs were present all throughout history, it remained a mystery to all of mankind. No one began to clue into what really was going on until after the resurrection of Jesus Christ. God took it upon Himself to do something for mankind that he could not do for himself. Taking responsibility means actively doing something about a problem or an issue, especially one that exists because of you. That's something we don't do enough, if at all. It doesn't mean just excusing it away with empty phrases like, "Oh well, nobody's perfect". That's quite obvious. Taking responsibility requires an action that attempts to rectify the situation. In the case of God, He did just that!

> [1]As for you, you were dead in your transgressions and sins, [2]in which you used to live when you followed the ways of this world and of the ruler of the kingdom of the air, the spirit who is now at work in those who are disobedient. [3]All of us also lived among them at one time, gratifying the cravings of our sinful nature and following its desires and thoughts. Like the rest, we were by nature objects of wrath. [4]But because of his great love for us, God, who is rich in mercy, [5]made us alive with Christ even when we were dead in transgressions – it is by grace you have been saved.
>
> (Ephesians 2:1-5)

In Paul's letter to the Christians in Ephesus, he begins to tell them what God has done for them. In order to help them have a better understanding and appreciation, he first gives them a description of their condition prior to God's intervention. He tells the Ephesians that they were dead in their transgressions and sins in which they used to live. This is a pretty interesting phrase, "dead in your transgressions and sins". In the Greek, the word for dead here is *nekros*. It means lifeless, deceased, or metaphorically speaking spiritually dead. Since Paul is writing to living, breathing people, we know that he's not talking about physical death, but spiritual death. This is someone who is destitute of a life that recognizes and is devoted to God because they are given over to their trespasses and sins. They have absolutely no contact whatsoever with God. Now, to get a better understanding, let's entertain this question for a minute from the perspective of physical death. What can a dead man do? Didn't need the full minute to answer that one did you? Absolutely nothing is what a dead man is capable of doing. He is completely devoid of life and cannot attain it on his own. Someone with their thinking cap on may get creative and say that he can stink up the place if he lies around for too long. I would have to agree with that answer as well. You're probably wondering, what kind of a silly question is this. But, you'll understand the importance of my asking this silly question here in just a second. After disclosing some other facts regarding their prior condition, he reveals to them that it was out of God's great love for them that He made them spiritually alive with Christ. Salvation is the work of God and God alone. Mankind has done absolutely nothing and can do nothing in regard to his spiritual condition. There's nothing he can take credit for because there's nothing that he could have done. Now's the time to refer back to the silly question that I asked a brief moment ago to solidify the point that Paul was making with the Ephesians. Remember the answer? A dead man can do absolutely nothing. As for stinking up the place, this describes us perfectly when we live according to our sinful nature. Take a look at all of the depraved things that people are doing in the world. An Australian man holds his daughter captive for twenty-four years while he constantly rapes her and fathers her seven children, another man shoots two rounds into a McDonald's drive-through window simply because the

McDonald's was not serving lunch yet. And it only gets worse as time goes by. Well, you might say, "I thought you said that we have free will. I know there's something we can take credit for." In answer to that, take a gander back at verse 3 of the Ephesians passage. After Paul tells them that they were dead in their transgressions, he tells them, inclusive of himself, exactly what they did while they were dead in their transgressions. He says, "All of us also lived among them at one time, gratifying the cravings of our sinful nature and following its desires and thoughts. Like the rest, we were by nature objects of wrath." Man's free will only pertain to the freedom of which sin they choose to indulge in and to what degree they indulge. Every person who has walked the face of the Earth, with the exception of Christ, has a sinful nature. Each person's sinful nature has a multitude of things that it craves. Some of those things become a major part of who we are as a person while others are not so much a part of who we are. Because of our helplessness, whatever our nature desires, we will take action to fulfill those desires. For those traits that are dominant, we become enslaved and are driven by their need for fulfillment. As a person indulges those dominant traits of their sinful nature, this, in many cases, will give birth to other sins. Take an individual who has become addicted to drugs. Depending on their situation at the time of addiction, they may use their own resources to support their habit. Once those resources have become exhausted, they resort to stealing anything from money to valuables they can easily sell in order to maintain the addiction. Whether it's family, friends, or a complete stranger, they'll steal from anyone who has anything of value. If resistance is so much even anticipated by the addict, murder can easily become the outcome. As you can see, sin breeds sin and some naturally travel together in packs like wolves. Some sins are easily visible while others are hidden and difficult to detect (I Timothy 5:24). The degree to which we are influenced by a particular sin varies from individual to individual. What I mean is this. The actions of one person may be different or more extreme than another while the root cause for those actions is identical. Hatred, for example, in one individual may cause prejudice while in another it produces a mass murderer. One is just as wrong as the other, but there's a big difference in the amount of damage and pain caused by the actions of the individuals. I anticipate that many would disagree or have a problem with the fact that both are equally as wrong as the other. The majority of the population would probably say that the mass murderer is more morally wrong than the prejudiced individual because it's more impactful. It is more impactful because it causes more damage, but this is purely humanistic thinking. I believe that there are two aspects of human nature that cause us to think in that way. First is the level at which we reason. We fail miserably at looking deep enough to find the source or explanation for our actions. In my previous example, we neglect to look into the depths of the heart to see the sin of hatred behind the actions of both individuals. In order to find out how this hatred was acquired, you'd have to draw out the character, the past environment, and the experiences of the individual. Despite the form and the degree to which it manifests itself, sin is still destructive. It causes pain and destroys relationships. Contrary to our lack of dealing with the heart, God always looks at the heart and is fully aware of its contents (I Samuel 16:7, John 2:24-25). Jesus was doing just that in the Sermon on the Mount when He says, "that anyone who looks at a woman lustfully has already committed adultery with her in his heart (Matthew 5:28)." Jesus confirms that adultery, the action, is wrong (v27), but what He's really trying to hit home with His audience is that the process started way before the action became a reality. Deep in the depths of the heart is where the action was conceived, and, as with all sin, is where it needs to be dealt with. That's how we, as disciples, are able to resist the temptation to sin because the cross of Christ has impacted our hearts. Prior to Jesus' speech, people were only focused on outward actions and this new teaching of Jesus was a difficult concept for them to grasp which is not a far stretch from how we are today. In addition to our short-sightedness, another downfall is that we have a tendency to look at things in terms of degrees to determine morally appropriate behavior. As we decide what's right and wrong for ourselves, we typically deem any unacceptable actions in excess of our own as being wrong, thus, making anything within our behavioral boundaries acceptable. But God sees this from an absolutely different perspective and you best believe that His perspective is going to prevail. Romans 3 says, "There is no difference, for all have sinned and fall short of the glory of God." In His eyes, sin is sin. The specific detail of what we've done doesn't matter. We've all sinned leaving us equally as guilty as any other.

Without Christ, we earn what we so diligently worked for (Romans 6:23). Now, for a change of pace, how did God make us alive with Christ?

> [21]To this you were called, because Christ suffered for you, leaving you an example, that you should follow in his steps. [22]"He committed no sin, and no deceit was found in his mouth." [23]When they hurled their insults at him, he did not retaliate; when he suffered, he made no threats. Instead, he entrusted himself to him who judges justly. [24]He himself bore our sins in his body on the tree, so that we might die to sins and live for righteousness; by his wounds you have been healed. [25]For you were like sheep going astray, but now you have returned to the Shepherd and Overseer of your souls.
>
> (I Peter 2:21-25)

Jesus suffered at the hands of men so that you wouldn't have to suffer the wrath of God for eternity. Just as a prisoner on death row can only wait for his time to be executed, so is the life of man without Jesus Christ before God. Jesus took our rightful place under the wrath of God so that those who would choose to follow Him would inherit His righteousness and live. I'm reminded of the jewelry that I see people wearing around their necks, the films, and paintings that only capture a token portion, if much at all, of the sufferings of Christ. In my personal opinion, "The Passion of the Christ" depicts the sufferings of Christ more than anything that I've seen in my lifetime. Yet, it still doesn't come within light-years of capturing the totality of Jesus' sufferings. Isaiah the prophet says that Jesus' "appearance was so disfigured beyond that of any man and his form marred beyond human likeness..." Can you fathom someone beaten so badly that you can't even recognize the fact that they are a human being? Although attempts can be made to more reflect the reality of Jesus' physical sufferings, there are three things that I see from the above passage that we'll never be able to capture. They are His innocence, the burden of carrying the sins of the world, and His motivation behind enduring such suffering.

Jesus suffered undeservingly. This is the example that He left for us to follow. We are to suffer undeservingly, to be blameless and above reproach. It requires living a life free of sin (not being without sin but being characterized by it) because Jesus was without sin. He was pure, evidenced by the lack of deceit found in His mouth (I Peter 2:21-22, Matthew 12:33-34). Have you ever suffered for something you didn't do? How did you feel? Hurt? Angry? Mistreated? I remember a time from my childhood when my mother and I were living in Jennings, Louisiana with my grandmother. I was in the fourth or fifth grade at the time. Being that we moved in the middle of the school year, I had to go through being the "strange" kid in class for the first time in my life. Man, was that a drag! Not to mention that I was quiet and didn't make friends very easily. Now, maybe I was asking a bit too much, but you would think that the teacher would do what she could do to help make me feel as comfortable as possible in, for a kid, a stressful situation. Yet, this woman began to criticize me relentlessly shortly after I was there. As time progressed, she called me names and told me that I had made all kinds of bad grades on my assignments. My little self-esteem was being battered and maimed; I was crushed and didn't know what to do. The only thing I could do was tell my mother, who taught me if someone (an adult) bothered me, I should let her know. So, that's just what I did. It was seemingly every day that I went home and told my mother something cruel that my teacher had said to me. Finally, my mother had had enough and decided it was time to go up to that school and have a one-on-one with the teacher to find out what was going on. Upon entering the classroom, the class had already started, so I immediately went to my desk in the back of the room while my mother stayed in the front to speak with the teacher. As I awaited the outcome, I began to feel as though we were going to get to the bottom of this. Freedom was about to ring and the phrase made famous by Dr. King seemed to fill the air, at least in my mind it did. "Free at last, free at last, thank God Almighty, I'm free at last." I saw the teacher walk over to her desk, grab her grade book, and walk back over to where my mother was standing. I continued to watch the inaudible conversation between the teacher and my mother, and it became apparent to me that things were going severely astray. After my mother looked into the teacher's grade book, she looked up at me with this very angry expression on her face. She, then, beckoned me to meet her outside the classroom. She chewed me out mercilessly and promised me that when I got home, I was going to get the spanking that I'd never forget. Now, this wasn't exactly the outcome that I had anticipated and was baffled as to how it took a sudden turn for the worse. I didn't deserve what was in store for me and was feeling rather confused, defeated, and helpless. I was angry with the teacher and even more so at my mother because she knew me better than that. That was not the type of behavior that I exhibited. She didn't call me over to try to rectify the situation. After all of this, I still had to go back in the classroom to face embarrassment, the teacher, and the constant thought of the only thing I had to look forward to at the end of the day was this spanking that came with a guarantee to be one that I'll never forget. I didn't think that guarantee was really necessary being that I was confident that I had some pretty memorable ones already under my belt. So, I wasn't particularly looking forward to going home to meet this one. Well, when I entered the room, the teacher sneered at me in her usual way and called me a little liar and rattled off some other verbiage that I couldn't understand as she walked back to her desk. At this point, I felt like taking my little Pro Wings and sticking them somewhere they didn't belong. I was pretty upset. And, as you can probably imagine, this was an unbelievably long day. I had hoped that somehow it all was just a bad dream. But, to my dismay, when I got home, Mom made good on her promise. When I got home, I found out from my mother that the grades she saw for me were all A's and B's. She said that she was shocked when she saw the grades. I thought she had her nerves to be shocked, believe me; I was just as shocked as she was when I heard them. Obviously, after what I had been telling her, she thought that I had lied. Throughout the whole situation, I was so overwhelmed with anger and a wealth of other emotions. I really felt like retaliating against everybody, my mother, the teacher, and even my fellow classmates. Now, in the case of Jesus, on top of all that He endured through, He once never retaliated or threatened us (v23). I'm in no way saying that my little childhood experience was equivocal to what Jesus suffered but think about it. How hard was that to do? How hard is it not to fight back and plead your case when you're innocent? Heck, we do that most times when we're clearly in the wrong! One thing I've become thoroughly convinced of from this is that by our brutal treatment of Jesus, His innocence showed just how wretched we truly are. I'm reminded of the old English idiom, "birds of a feather flock together." Quite naturally, when you look at the group, you won't notice much difference between the individuals that make up the group because they're all pretty much the same. The same holds true for depraved mankind. You have a bunch of wicked beings doing wicked things to each other and when you look at the group, you don't notice much difference. As a matter of fact, you can probably justify some of the bad things that happen. For instance, if someone breaks into your home to rob you and gets shot and killed in the process, what's the response? Yes, that is an unfortunate thing to have happen to another human being, but they shouldn't have been breaking into your home in the first place. Now, throw Jesus into the mix of the group and how we treated Him. What did Jesus do to deserve such mistreatment? He helped a multitude of people, the very people who hung Him on a cross and murdered Him. He healed the sick and fed the poor, and He ended up being treated worse than any other man in the history of the world.

When Jesus was up on that cross, He had the sins of the entire world upon Him. What was it like to bear such a burden? I think of my own sins and how it affected me and each individual involved. I think of the hurt, the separation, and the damage that each person walked away with and carried for the rest of their lives. Imagine one person absorbing all of that for the entire population that has ever lived and ever will live (Isaiah 53:4-6). I don't think the human mind has the capacity to fully grasp that concept. We only experience sin in incremental amounts. That is when we sin against another, ourselves, or another sin against us. I recall a time several years ago reminiscing about conversations I had with some ex-girlfriends. I don't know what prompted me to recall this. Maybe I was watching the news or something, but I remembered conversations about their experiences being sexually molested as children. As I thought about this, I couldn't help but give way to the thought that this happens far more than I could possibly imagine. It was frustrating as I wondered how many people were walking around that had been damaged by this heinous crime. Now, this was only one type of offense. Include the many other ways that we inflict each other, and you have a thought that's pretty unbearable. We are all just a bunch of self-inflicted individuals adept at causing each other more pain and grief. Jesus is the only one who can provide compensation for every one of our sins. Although Jesus paid for the sins of the world by dying on the cross, an individual's sins aren't paid for until they surrender and turn themselves in to Him.

Let's explore briefly the relationship between a shepherd and his sheep to discover the motivation behind Jesus enduring His hardships and suffering. A characteristic of sheep is that they are prey animals by nature. It's a very natural expectation that they are going to be attacked. Sheep would probably have a complex if, all of a sudden, they weren't attacked anymore. How would you like that kind of lifestyle? They are a primary source of food for many other animals, which means they are attacked quite often. When a predator invades their flight zone, they have limited resources for defending themselves. They rely heavily upon evasion and meager "fight" tactics such as hoof stamping or displaying aggressive postures when cornered as a means of protecting themselves. In addition to being a primary source of food for predatory animals, sheep are beneficial to humans as well and are in desperate need of constant protection if we are to receive that benefit. This is where the shepherd comes in. The duties of a shepherd are to watch for enemies trying to attack the sheep, to defend the sheep from attackers, to heal the wounded and sick sheep, to find and save lost or trapped sheep, and to share their lives and earn their trust. Why would the shepherd go to all of that trouble and risk his life for the sheep? As Jesus contrasts the actions of the good shepherd, referring to Himself, and the hired hand, He tells us in John 10 that the hired hand flees when danger comes because he cares nothing for the flock whereas the good shepherd does. Jesus' motivation for dying for mankind was rooted out of a deep love for him. He saw man's predicament and his inability to remove himself from his situation and Jesus, out of His great love for us gave His life in exchange for ours. He did this with the full knowledge of the fact that there would be many who would reject Him. How would a hurdle like that affect the motivation you had for accomplishing a task? Even with this in mind, Jesus still completed His task. The lesson to learn is that true love requires a willingness to risk, sacrifice, and endure hardships for the benefit of the other including those who are the most unloving. This is what got Jesus through all of the sufferings that He faced on our behalf.

Jesus experienced an immense amount of physical, emotional, and spiritual suffering that would have long broken the ordinary man. We're now going to traverse through Jesus' life in the hours leading up to His crucifixion. While we do that, I encourage you to get personal with it. Put yourself in His shoes and think about how you would respond as I paint a picture of a few things that might not come to mind as you read through the passages.

> [20]When evening came, Jesus was reclining at the table with the Twelve. [21]And while they were eating, he said, "I tell you the truth, one of you will betray me." [22]They were very sad and began to say to him one after the other, "Surely not I, Lord?" [23]Jesus replied, "The one who has dipped his hand into the bowl with me will betray me. [24]The Son of Man will go just as it is written about him. But woe to that man who betrays the Son of Man! It would be better for him if he had not been born." [25]Then Judas, the one who would betray him, said, "Surely not I, Rabbi?" Jesus answered, "Yes, it is you."
>
> (Matthew 26:20-25)

Jesus is here eating the Passover meal with His twelve disciples, and He begins to tell them out of the blue that one of them was going to betray Him. This saddens the disciples and one after the other they began to exclaim, "Surely not I, Lord?" Finally, Judas Iscariot responds, "Surely not I, Rabbi", but Jesus confirms that he is the culprit. In lying directly to Jesus' face, Judas hints at the fact that he didn't feel quite the same about Jesus as the rest of the disciples. The eleven disciples referred to Jesus as Lord while Judas merely saw Jesus as a teacher. In verses 14-16, Judas had already put his plan into action to betray Jesus. He had gone to the chief priests and received payment of the thirty silver coins. It is very likely that Judas had the money on him when he lied to Jesus' face. Jesus knew Judas was lying to Him. How do you think Jesus felt knowing Judas was lying to Him? Has a friend ever lied to your face and you knew it? What did you think about it? How did you feel? How did you respond? Did that change your attitude about that person? If so, how? Think about this for a moment. Jesus always knew that Judas would be the one to betray Him from the very beginning. Despite knowing this piece of information, Jesus still hung out and shared meals with this guy. He poured His heart out to Judas without reserve and treated him no different than the other disciples. Could you have done that with anyone? I know I couldn't have even come close to achieving that with anyone. This shows the depth of Jesus' love. He loved others unconditionally whether they loved Him in return or not. Have you ever loved like that? Jesus loves you in the exact same manner.

> [31]Then Jesus told them, "This very night you will all fall away on account of me, for it is written: 'I will strike the shepherd, and the sheep of the flock will be scattered.' [32]But after I have risen, I will go ahead of you into Galilee." [33]Peter replied, "Even if all fall away on account of you, I never will." [34]"I tell you the truth, " Jesus answered, "this very night, before the rooster crows, you will disown me three times." [35]But Peter declared, "Even if I have to die with you, I will never disown you." And all the other disciples said the same.
>
> (Matthew 26:31-35)

Ever been called a liar to your face when you knew you were telling the truth? Recall the feelings that you had? That's essentially what's going on here. Not long after being lied to by Judas, Peter opposes Jesus to His face. By his actions, he calls Jesus a liar as though He doesn't know what He's talking about. Why would Peter do this? At this point in their relationship, he clearly knew who Jesus was? This wasn't the first time Peter had opposed Jesus (Matthew 16:13-23). In his pride and deceitfulness regarding his own heart, Peter pledges this allegiance to Jesus that he would soon falter on. He said it with such conviction that he led the others to believe that they too would follow suit. You would think that Peter would have learned from his previous experience of opposing Jesus. In addition to the fact that he truly knew who Jesus was, you'd think that Jesus' comment would have prompted a different response from Peter this time around. This goes to show the impact that our sin can have on us as well as others. We can become so steeped in sin to the point where what is sensible is not sensible and what is not sensible makes perfect sense. Let me provide you with a little example of what I'm talking about. There's a particular radio personality who has made some pretty detrimental comments regarding the president and his socialistic plan for getting the American economy back on its feet. The comment made by this particular individual stated, in summary, that he wanted Obama and his plans to fail because he wanted America to succeed. The first thought that came to my mind was, "What on Earth is this guy talking about? Does he reside in another country or something?" I'm thinking does he not realize that the president's failure will affect America and him too? That doesn't make sense! That's like saying I hope Phil Jackson fails as a coach so that the Los Angeles Lakers can be successful. If the coach fails, the whole organization fails. The same goes for the president and the United States. This guy is definitely not thinking clearly. I'm not saying that he has to agree with everything the president does, but to make a statement like that is absolute nonsense. I'd have to say that there's some animosity lurking just beneath the surface.

> ³⁶Then Jesus went with his disciples to a place called Gethsemane, and he said to them, "Sit here while I go over there and pray." ³⁷He took Peter and the two sons of Zebedee along with him, and he began to be sorrowful and troubled. ³⁸Then he said to them, "My soul is overwhelmed with sorrow to the point of death. Stay here and keep watch with me." ³⁹Going a little farther, he fell with his face to the ground and prayed, "My Father, if it is possible, may this cup be taken from me. Yet not as I will, but as you will." ⁴⁰Then he returned to his disciples and found them sleeping. "Could you men not keep watch with me for one hour?" he asked Peter. ⁴¹"Watch and pray so that you will not fall into temptation. The spirit is willing, but the body is weak." ⁴²He went away a second time and prayed, "My Father, if it is not possible for this cup to be taken away unless I drink it, may your will be done." ⁴³When he came back, he again found them sleeping, because their eyes were heavy. ⁴⁴So he left them and went away once more and prayed the third time, saying the same thing. ⁴⁵Then he returned to the disciples and said to them, "Are you still sleeping and resting? Look, the hour is near, and the Son of Man is betrayed into the hands of sinners. ⁴⁶Rise, let us go! Here comes my betrayer!"
>
> (Matthew 26:36-46)

They say that in times of trouble, you find out who your friends truly are. Those are the ones who stick by your side through thick and thin. At the most agonizing time in His life up to this point, Jesus was without the support of His closest friends. While He prayed to God for strength in preparation for His crucifixion, Peter, James, and John couldn't even be by His side to pray with Him. Have you ever been abandoned by a friend at a time when you needed him or her the most? I bet it changed your whole view of them, didn't it? I recall a time when I was high school age and playing basketball at the neighborhood playground. Sometimes, you can get in what they call the "zone." It's a state where you're absolutely unstoppable. The basket seemed like the Pacific Ocean, and the ball seemed like a pebble. No matter what anybody does to try and stop you, it turns out to be detrimental to them. Every athlete has had a few days like this and that day was definitely one for me. My teammates immediately gave me the ball and literally stood back and watched. I remember a couple of times after I had scored a basket, I went back to play defense only to realize that not one of them had ever crossed half court. Well, a couple of guys on the other team weren't as appreciative of the display of basketball skills as my teammates were. So, on one occasion, after I scored and headed back down the court, one of the guys threw the basketball at me, hitting me in the back of my head. I went from excitement to anger all in a hot second. The two of us exchanged words, and before you knew it, we were fighting. As I began to get the best of this guy, his partner crept up behind me. He grabbed my arms just as the other guy happened to swing. The punch landed right on the front of my mouth, knocking out one tooth and leaving another hanging by the roots. So, now, I'm in between these two guys, throwing and taking punches, back and forth until the fight all of a sudden comes to a complete halt. Then, everybody just walks away. What I haven't revealed about this story that makes it significant to my point is that two of my family members were there watching the whole thing unfold and never once lifted a finger to help me once the fight became lopsided. I had helped them and stood up for them before, and here they leave me out in the cold. As I walked home, with the two of them by my side, I was very angry with them. I really didn't want them walking home with me. I felt like beating the daylights out of them but didn't even so much bother scolding them. I was more concerned with getting home so that I could get to the hospital to get the attention that I needed. A lesson to learn in all this is that people are going to let you down whether intentionally or unintentionally and sometimes in the worst way imaginable. We're all a bunch of imperfect beings, and we must learn to accept and deal with this fact in a constructive manner.

> [47]While he was still speaking, Judas, one of the Twelve, arrived. With him was a large crowd armed with swords and clubs, sent from the chief priests and the elders of the people. [48]Now the betrayer had arranged a signal with them: "The one I kiss is the man; arrest him." [49]Going at once to Jesus, Judas said, "Greetings, Rabbi!" and kissed him. [50]Jesus replied, "Friend, do what you came for." Then the men stepped forward, seized Jesus and arrested him.
>
> (Matthew 26:47-50)

After Jesus finishes praying, Judas is approaching with a large crowd ready to arrest Him. Judas walks up to Jesus as though nothing is wrong, probably smiling at Him as he betrays Him with a kiss. Betrayal by a friend is a pretty serious thing to have done to you, especially right there in front of your face. Jesus' response to Judas amazes me simply because I couldn't imagine myself responding to him as a friend in any form or fashion. On top of all that, remember, Jesus knew beforehand that Judas would be the one to betray Him. Out of love and His willingness to fulfill God's will (v54), Jesus was willing to associate and endure this type of treatment from Judas. Finally, in verse 56, we see Jesus' prediction come to light as He is physically abandoned by the remaining disciples even after they each pledged they'd be by His side to the end.

> [57]Those who had arrested Jesus took him to Caiaphas, the high priest where the teachers of the law and the elders had assembled. [58]But Peter followed him at a distance, right up to the courtyard of the high priest. He entered and sat down with the guards to see the outcome. [59]The chief priests and the whole Sanhedrin were looking for false evidence against Jesus so that they could put him to death. [60]But they did not find any, though many false witnesses came forward. Finally, two came forward [61]and declared, "This fellow said, 'I am able to destroy the temple of God and rebuild it in three days.'" [62]Then the high priest stood up and said to Jesus, "Are you not going to answer? What is this testimony that these men are bringing against you?" [63]But Jesus

remained silent. The high priest said to him, "I charge you under oath by the living God: Tell us if you are the Christ, the Son of God." [64]"Yes, it is as you say," Jesus replied. "But I say to all of you: In the future you will see the Son of Man sitting at the right hand of the Mighty One and coming on the clouds of heaven." [65]Then the high priest tore his clothes and said, "He has spoken blasphemy! Why do we need any more witnesses? Look, now you have heard the blasphemy. [66]What do you think?" "He is worthy of death," they answered. [67]Then they spit in his face and struck him with their fists. Others slapped him and said, "Prophesy to us, Christ. Who hit you?"

(Matthew 26:57-67)

Jesus is now on trial before the Sanhedrin, which is the Jewish high court, equivalent to our Supreme Court. Here, the hatred of the people towards Jesus begins to escalate as they have conspired to have Jesus sentenced to death. Many people stepped up to bring false accusations against Jesus, but nothing stuck because of the lack of matching testimonies (Mark 14:55-56). Under the Jewish laws, a man could only be put to death on the testimony of two or three people (Deuteronomy 17:6). Just think for a moment about what type of feelings would emerge from watching people knowingly telling lies against you? Finally, two from the crowd spoke up quoting a statement Jesus made earlier in regard to destroying and rebuilding the temple. The meaning of the quote was obviously misconstrued, although it's not clear whether it was by ignorance or intention (John 2:19-21). Following Jesus' reply to the high priest, the wickedness of man had run its course. Jesus was charged with blasphemy and sentenced to death. I can't begin to fathom what it must feel like to be sentenced to death in a court of law for something that you did not do. After the verdict, the people began spitting in His face, hitting Him with their fists, and mocking Him. Jesus was treated inhumanely by the people He was here to save. Imagine having a crowd of people taking turns spitting in your face. Being drenched in saliva as others took their turn punching you. Think about the physical pain you would feel, the swelling of your face, the overwhelming feelings of humiliation and degradation.

> [69]Now Peter was sitting out in the courtyard, and a servant girl came to him. "You also were with Jesus of

> Galilee," she said. ⁷⁰But he denied it before them all. "I don't know what you're talking about," he said. ⁷¹Then he went out to the gateway, where another girl saw him and said to the people there, "This fellow was with Jesus of Nazareth." ⁷²He denied it again, with an oath: "I don't know the man!" ⁷³After a little while, those standing there went up to Peter and said, "Surely you are one of them, for your accent gives you away." ⁷⁴Then he began to call down curses on himself and he swore to them, "I don't know the man!" Immediately a rooster crowed. ⁷⁵Then Peter remembered the word Jesus had spoken: "Before the rooster crows, you will disown me three times." And he went outside and wept bitterly.
>
> (Matthew 26:69-75)

Peter, who had followed Jesus at a distance, saw what had just happened and didn't lift a finger to help Jesus, even after he solemnly swore complete allegiance to Him. Peter, who was one of Jesus' best friends out of the Twelve, fulfills what Jesus had warned him of earlier. He denied ever knowing Jesus three times, twice to a mere servant girl. During the final denial, Peter became so indignant that he became belligerent and swore that he didn't know Jesus. At that moment, the rooster crowed, and Peter is reminded of what Jesus had said. What really tears your heart out is the fact that when the rooster crowed, Jesus turned and caught Peter's eye (Luke 22:60-62).

Can you imagine the flood of emotions that welled up? How would you feel watching your best friend deny ever knowing you with some strong exclamations? This is a person that you've grown very close to. You've poured your heart out and invested in this person. Then, in return, they betray you practically to your face. This would be equivalent to having a child grow up and boldly deny his or her parents after being nurtured, taught, provided, and cared for by them his or her entire life. Up to this point, Jesus has endured a lot and hadn't even gotten to the cross yet.

> [11]Meanwhile Jesus stood before the governor, and the governor asked him, "Are you the king of the Jews?" "Yes, it is as you say," Jesus replied. [12]When he was accused by the chief priests and the elders, he gave no answer. [13]Then Pilate asked him, "Don't you hear the testimony they are bringing against you?" [14]But Jesus made no reply, not even to a single charge – to the great amazement of the governor. [15]Now it was the governor's custom at the Feast to release a prisoner chosen by the crowd. [16]At that time they had a notorious prisoner, called Barabbas. [17]So when the crowd had gathered, Pilate asked them, "Which one do you want me to release to you: Barabbas, or Jesus who is called Christ?" [18]For he knew it was out of envy that they had handed Jesus over to him. [19]While Pilate was sitting on the judge's seat, his wife sent him this message: "Don't have anything to do with that innocent man, for I have

> suffered a great deal today in a dream because of him." ²⁰But the chief priests and the elders persuaded the crowd to ask for Barabbas and to have Jesus executed. ²¹"Which of the two do you want me to release to you?" asked the governor. "Barabbas," they answered. ²²"What shall I do, then, with Jesus who is called Christ?" Pilate asked. They all answered, "Crucify him!" ²³"Why? What crime has he committed?" asked Pilate. But they shouted all the louder, "Crucify him!" ²⁴When Pilate saw that he was getting nowhere, but that instead an uproar was starting, he took water and washed his hands in front of the crowd. "I am innocent of this man's blood," he said. "It is your responsibility!" ²⁵All the people answered, "Let his blood be on us and on our children!" ²⁶Then he released Barabbas to them. But he had Jesus flogged, and handed him over to be crucified.
>
> (Matthew 27:11-26)

Jesus has now been turned over to Pontius Pilate, the Roman governor, to have his execution carried out. Under the Roman government, the Sanhedrin was deprived of the right to carry out capital punishment. So again, Jesus is on trial and facing the murderous intentions of the large crowd. They are treating Jesus worse than a common criminal. They shout to have Barabbas, a notorious criminal, released and to have Jesus crucified. What did Jesus do to deserve being treated this way? Maybe it was because of the many people that He had healed.

Or, maybe it was because of those He had raised from the dead. Or maybe, it was because of the five thousand He had fed with two fish and five loaves of bread. If not those, surely, it had to be because of the grace He extended to those who came to Him because He wanted them to know God and have peace in their lives. Can you imagine standing before the very people you devoted three years of your life to helping as you listened to them scream at the top of their lungs in favor of your death? "Crucify him, crucify him", they exuberantly shouted until Pilate finally gave in. Think about this for a moment. If you are being falsely accused, no matter the situation, and someone there knows your innocence, wouldn't you expect them to take a stand and speak up on your behalf especially if they had the influence to sway the others? How would you feel if they didn't? Pilate found no fault with Jesus (v23) and had the power to free Jesus, but instead sold Jesus out to the crowd. He handed Him over to be flogged and crucified. For those of you who aren't familiar with what flogging is, here's a brief description for you. In a flogging, a whip was used to punish criminals. This whip had several leather straps attached to the handle. Embedded at the end of the straps were various types of sharp objects proficient at tearing human flesh. The objects could be anything such as lead, bones, spikes, hooks, or metal. The individual being punished would be tied up and bent over so that his back would be exposed. As they were being whipped, the sharp objects would stick in and tear the flesh off the back of the individual as the executioner swung the whip back for another lashing. As the beating progressed, muscle and meat would be torn as well. It was customary amongst the Jews to limit the number of lashes to forty. In case of a miscount, they practiced counting to thirty-nine. Now, the Romans, on the other hand, had no such limitations. As a result, floggings at the hands of the Romans were so brutal that many criminals died during the floggings and never made it to the crucifixion. Jesus was flogged at the hands of the Romans.

> ^{27}Then the governor's soldiers took Jesus into the Praetorium and gathered the whole company of soldiers around him. ^{28}They stripped him and put a scarlet robe on him, ^{29}and then twisted together a crown of thorns and set it on his head. They put a staff in his right hand and knelt in front of him and mocked him. "Hail, king of the Jews!" they said. ^{30}They spit on him, and took the staff and struck him on the head again and again. ^{31}After they had mocked him, they took off the robe and put his own clothes on him. Then they led him away to crucify him.
>
> (Matthew 27:27-31)

After being flogged to within inches away from death, Jesus' condition is pretty severe. His back has been literally shredded. He is extremely weak from desanguination, and the pain He feels is very excruciating and unbearable. As if He hasn't already experienced enough, He is taken by some soldiers into the Praetorium where the entire company of soldiers inflicts more pain, insults, and humiliation on Him. Bleeding profusely, the soldiers put a robe on Him only to rip it away from His wounds later, which reopens the wounds to cause more bleeding and pain. They put a crown of thorns on His head and continue to spit on Him. They used the staff they gave Him to strike Him on the head, embedding those thorns even deeper into the sensitive area of the scalp. All of this and Jesus still hadn't made it to the cross. Why would He endure through such suffering and punishment?

> [45]From the sixth hour until the ninth hour darkness came over all the land. [46]About the ninth hour Jesus cried out in a loud voice, "Eloi, Eloi, lama sabachthani?" – which means, "My God, my God, why have you forsaken me?"
>
> (Matthew 27:45-46)

Approximately nine hours since being arrested and on top of all of the punishment He has already endured, Jesus has now been crucified. Nails have been driven through the medial nerves in His hands and through His feet. Being that the victim's body wasn't fully extended when crucified, Jesus is in a constant struggle between searching for a comfortable position and finding relief from the stress on the nerves in His hands and feet. This is compounded greatly by the need to take a breath. Jesus is in a vicious cycle between lifting His body with His weight supported by His weaken legs and letting His body slump with His weight being supported by the nails driven through His wrists. While He goes through this process, the wounds on His back from the flogging He received earlier are reopened and aggravated over and over again. The nerves are aggravated again as His back rubs against the wooden post, and splinters begin to lodge in His back, which is already beyond the bearable point of tenderness and sensitivity. Jesus has been in constant pain and bleeding for several hours now. Immediately before giving up His life, He cries out loudly to God asking why He has forsaken Him. Why do you think Jesus would ask this question? Especially, now. This is the point in time when Jesus had the sins of the world on His shoulders, which resulted in Him being separated from God. The burden of Jesus carrying the sins of the world was not a physical burden, but a spiritual one. This was the first time in all eternity that He had been separated from God. Although He was away physically while He walked the Earth, Jesus still had a very unique relationship with God the Father. But on that cross, all ties to the Father were severed, and Jesus was completely shut out from the presence of God, which is literally the essence of hell (II Thessalonians 1:8-9). If Jesus felt this troubled about being separated from God, then, how much more should we?

Behold, this is not the end of the story. Christ rose from the dead and lives! Jesus did all of this as a provision for all of mankind. But only to those who decide to trust Him and faithfully follow in His footsteps, Jesus provides eternal life, a means for escaping the eternal suffering that we were once assured of. He is the passageway into heaven (John 3:16).

Jesus has given us confidence that we may approach the throne to receive His mercy and help (Hebrews 4:15-16). We have confidence knowing that Jesus, our Great High Priest, was tempted in every way that we are. We can rest assured that He understands and sympathizes with what we are experiencing because He has gone through the same sufferings. What an amazing thought – a Savior, a God that wants to endure through our trials and sufferings with us hand in hand every step of the way. This is what fuels our confidence in persevering through any kind of trial, tragedy, and tribulation. We have a Savior who has already been through the war, and He is at the right hand of God interceding on our behalf (Romans 8:34).

Jesus has opened our eyes to see the glory that lies beyond the boundaries of this world (Romans 8:18). We are motivated and strengthened to persist through our present sufferings by the very thought of spending eternity in heaven with God. That's exactly what we have to look forward to. In fact, Paul told the Ephesians that they were seated with Christ in the heavenly realms (Ephesians 2:6-7). As we live our earthly lives, we are (spiritually speaking) already presently residing in heaven through our union and exaltation with Christ. What an amazing thought! The bad we experience here doesn't even come close to comparing with the glorious riches that are waiting for us in heaven. Knowing this, what other motivation do you need? This is the example that Christ clearly left behind. For, He had the exact same motivation as He endured through His sufferings while here on Earth (Hebrews 12:2).

Christ lived in and overcame the world. Therefore, in Christ, we are more than conquerors (Romans 8:37). Through the Holy Spirit, He gives us the right and power to overcome the world as He did. This means that we have been set free from the pernicious views, attitudes, and thinking of this present world in regards to our suffering. They only lead to feelings like self-pity, discouragement, and selfishness, which are counterproductive to God's purposes for suffering.

Because we know this one simple fact that in *all* things God works for the good of those who love Him – those who have been called according to His purpose (Romans 8:28). We can rest assured and trust that in every trial, every challenging situation, and every form of suffering, whether "how" ever becomes evident to us or not, that God is working it out for our good. The Almighty God has got my back – what is there for me to worry about? Who or what can be against me? Because of this valuable piece of information, we can be transformed in our thinking and our attitudes about suffering, even when in the midst of it. We can think, what is God trying to show me, instead of, why is this happening to me. We can be certain that God is in control and has a plan instead of thinking that our trials are merely arbitrary happenings that are only meant to inconvenience us and add stress to our lives. Now, imagine the change this kind of thinking will have on your life?

I hope that you have now gained some understanding as to what God has done about the problem of suffering. What is required of us is that we accept the gift by faith and commit ourselves to walk in His ways for the rest of our lives. God went to great lengths for you and me. He's done far more than He needed to do. Keep in mind that God didn't have to do what He did and would have been completely justified if He had decided not to. So, if it's not obvious by now, the next move is yours. And, the real question becomes, "What are you going to do?"

CHAPTER FOUR

Now What?

Hopefully, you were able to find some good information from what you've read. My thoughts are that good information is useless without some practical means of extracting some personal benefits from it. There are four suggestions that I'd like to discuss that can be beneficial to you when facing challenging situations if you would allow them to become a part of your life and strive to grow in them. This list is not, by any stretch of the imagination, considered to be a comprehensive list of suggestions. I hope that your eyes were opened to seeing things that I won't even mention. The things I'm going to share are merely some things that I've learned from my personal experiences that stood out after the fact. I know they would be really helpful if you'd consistently strive towards personally growing in them when you encounter trials and difficulties in our multi-faceted life.

As I think about my first suggestion and overall reason for writing this book, I am reminded of an email conversation that I had a few years ago at work with a friend of mine. This happens to be the same friend that I emailed regarding the encounter I had with my wife in the church parking lot. This particular conversation took place soon after my wife and I had separated. He asked me how life was going. I responded that it had its good points and its bad points. He quickly came back with, "Hopefully the good outweighs the bad." When I read that, something just didn't seem right about it. I thought for a brief moment or two and wrote the following response. "Instead of hoping that the good in our lives outweighs the bad, learning to always see the good in the midst of the bad would be much better. What we choose to see, which presents a challenge in itself, is what makes the difference in how we feel about the many challenges that go on in our daily lives." I would have never suspected something so deep could have come from the simplest of conversations. "Man, that was pretty profound", replied my friend as he began to elaborate on what he got out of the statement. As for me, I was pretty dumbfounded because that seemingly came out the middle of nowhere. I was totally caught off guard by my response, but it was really something to think about. Changing your perspective, choosing to see or being open to seeing other possibilities, will make a complete difference in your life. The Cambridge Dictionary defines perspective as a particular way of considering something. To get another perspective on the word, Wikipedia has it contextually defined as one's point of view, the choice of a context for opinions, beliefs, and experiences. Yet, another definition is a way of regarding situations or topics, the mental view or state of one's ideas. There are two major facts that stand out to me as I read through these definitions. The first of the two things is short and sweet. Perspective is a choice. It's not something that we're born with or given. It's something that we choose. It can and most likely will be influenced by our past experiences. It can be done consciously or subconsciously, but it's something that we do very frequently. And, most often than not, we don't recognize the decision we've made and its impact on how we see things from that point forward. The next thing is that our perspective is not the truth. Now, you wouldn't know this from the way we acted most times. You'd swear up and down that what we saw and how we saw it was the way that it was. As one of the definitions above puts it, it is *a way* of regarding something. Each of us can experience the same situation in many different ways. This is a result of our varying past experiences, the makeup of our characters, and the environment we grew up in. The problem with this is that we choose to see what we want to see and nothing else. We don't think about the fact that we don't see everything that evolves to make a situation play out the way it does or how the situation came to be in the first place. This was the foundation that the movie Vantage Point was built upon. This reminds me of a story that was told to me by a good friend of mine. It illustrates this concept to perfection. There were three guys who had been blind since birth. They were all friends, and neither of them knew what an elephant really was. They had heard stories of what they looked like but never really experienced it for themselves. One day, they decided that they were going to find out for themselves and would compare notes afterward. So, they got someone to take them to the zoo, and they went to the elephants. The first guy was at the front of the elephant and began to grab the elephant's trunk. He began saying to himself, "Elephants are round and slender." The second man came upon the elephant's ear and said to himself, "Elephants are leathery, flimsy, and really thin." The third guy was at the rear of the elephant and began to feel the elephant's leg. He thought, "Man, elephants are round and hard." When the three men came together, instead of comparing notes, they began arguing to no end about what an elephant was really like. Now, tell me, which of these guys were wrong? Neither of them was wrong. Each one only had a different experience with the elephant which influenced his perspective of the elephant. How do you think the situation would have changed if they had only experienced the elephant from one another's viewpoint? It would have been drastic. This brings me to the importance of why we should be eager to see situations from a perspective other than the one we typically jump to. When we're not, we cause divisions and quarrels. Imagine yourself about ready to play Final Jeopardy. This is the question that's going to make you or break you. As Alex Trebek poses his final question for the night, the entire place drops to a dead silence, and as he asks you, "Who does your perspective affect?" Can you hear the Jeopardy tune playing in the background? You reply, "Alex, who is me?" With exuberance, he says, "You are absolutely correct!" You may wreak havoc on another individual because of what you perceive, but ultimately, what you perceive affects only you. By choosing a perspective, you, in essence, are choosing a value system that is associated with what you believe to be true. This determines how you will behave when circumstances arise and how you interact with other individuals. I truly do believe that we can avoid a lot of drama in our lives if we were susceptible to the idea of seeing things from a different angle. Our relationships with each other, especially marriages, would be much better if we were willing to see the other person's point of view. It doesn't necessarily mean that we have to agree with them. Just listen. Think back to the three blind men and the elephant. We don't know a person's preconceived thoughts, how his or her day went up until that point, or we can go as far back as his or her childhood experiences that may have caused them to respond or view something the way they did. We may not always be able to experience something from the other person's viewpoint as in the example, but what we can do is try to understand. Trying to understand makes a far greater difference in the outcome than not trying. Also, we'd endure through tough situations better if we would be willing to see a brighter side or the good in the midst of the bad. Why is this? Because what we choose to see affects our attitude, and our behavior is a direct result of our attitude. So common sense tells me that if you want to change your behavior or how you respond to certain situations, then you must first change how you view those situations. Needless to say, this is much easier said than done. This is especially true if your survival is linked to the behavior. Changing one's perspective falls in accordance with the directive referenced earlier in I Peter 4:1. We are told that since Christ suffered, we are to arm ourselves with the same attitude. Now, this passage is specifically talking about suffering for doing righteous deeds, something that you didn't deserve (v3-4). This concept of arming ourselves is a critical one for us to grasp a hold of and can be incorporated into every situation that sets itself up as an obstacle in our lives. I've seen so many Christians get angry and fall away from God due to a trial or some tragedy that occurs in their life. If you think about this, its foolishness because He's the One who cared enough to warn you, and it's only through Him that you will endure through life's challenges. So, what does it mean to arm oneself? The Greek word *oplizo* means to furnish with arms, to provide, to furnish one's self with a thing, or metaphorically speaking, to take on the same mindset. In short, it means preparation. According to my experiences, if you have the luxury to be able to prepare yourself for something, this means that you have advance knowledge of its occurrence or its potential to occur. It's an inevitable event. What comes to my mind when I think of this is a soldier gearing up for war or a student cramming for his or her final exams. It would be a foolish thing for either one to enter into their respective situations without being properly equipped. Failure would then be inevitable and most likely immediate. The same concept applies to our sufferings. Why don't you gear up for it? You know that it's going to happen. It's just a matter of when and what. God's word is remarkable in that it never leaves us hanging. It gives us an example which to model ourselves after. This example is, of course, Jesus Christ. What was Christ's attitude towards His sufferings? On many occasions, Jesus foretold or made some reference to His impending sufferings. See the following: Matthew 12:40, 16:21, 17:12, 26:2, Mark 8:31, 9:12, Luke 9:22, 17:25, 22:15, 24:26, 24:46, & John 3:14-15. Jesus, with the full knowledge of exactly what and when He would have to suffer, faced them head-on with a willingness that wouldn't be thwarted. On too many occasions, I've seen just the opposite in my own character. In some things, if I catch an inkling of anything remotely challenging, my nature begins to sound off the alarm. It's time to take evasive actions! Depending on the situation, being shoved out of our comfort zones all of a sudden can be pretty challenging. I work as a software developer for a financial organization. There are many other aspects to my job, but what I like to do the most is write code. Just tell ole Clarence what it is you need done, and I'll sit down and write the code to do it. Yep, that's me! Just to clear up any misconceptions you may have formulated about me over the past three or four sentences. I'm not one of those types of people who just sit at a computer and write code all day long. I'm not one with the computer. I don't eagerly wait to leave work only to come home to write more code. In most instances, I'm just the opposite. I leave work, and I don't want to see another computer until I absolutely have to. That's typically the next day when I have to go back to work. Now, that I've cleared that up, I can continue on with my point (smile). A few years ago, I was loaned out to another project team where I was asked to fulfill the duties of the technical lead role. This responsibility had far less coding involved and required performing the necessary research to find all of the programs that needed to be changed to incorporate the new enhancements or functionality for the project. This required writing up documents that would specify all of the changes to each program. On top of that, I would "lead" or be the point man for the other programmers on the project. They would work from all of my findings and direction. Anyone who knows me well knows that this is totally out of my character and comfort zone. I absolutely did not want to do this. "Why can't someone else do this", I thought, even though I knew that I was the logical one for the job. The other two programmers on the project were contractors and didn't know the company's system or procedures as well as I did. I fought and wrestled with that in my heart for days. As I have felt in previous situations before, I, ultimately, felt incompetent to perform the tasks, and no matter what happened, it would result in me "being found out" to be a failure and, then I would be abolished from my job. Talk about living with a gun to your head. I have to admit that I also grumbled about the situation a bit to my project leader in one of our team meetings. Unfortunately, to no avail, there was no way around it. Being open with a friend about how I was feeling and knowing that there wasn't any escape, I began to change my attitude about it, and I eventually surrendered to the whole idea. I thought that if I was going to have to do this, then I might as well give my full heart, do the best that I can, and get the most out of it. This was far better than the alternative of not giving my heart at all, which would have led to me doing a half-hearted job resulting in a bad rapport amongst those working with me on the project. This would have been very bad for me when the time came for performance reviews or soliciting professional references for new job opportunities. This really turned out to be a good experience for me though. I would have spared myself a lot of drama and turmoil if I would have surrendered to begin with. Essentially, there's really not much difference with many of the other trials we face from day to day. A lot of what makes us or breaks us results from the mentality that we choose to have in the beginning. That's what has to change in order to bring about success no matter the circumstances.

As we transition over to the next point, we could think about this question to set ourselves up, "How was Christ so prepared for His trials?" Looking back at the passage from I Peter 2, we find the answer to this question. When Christ was confronted with the murderous threats of the hostile crowd, He didn't take matters into His own hands but entrusted Himself to Him who judges justly (v23). The word for entrusted in Greek is the word *paradidomi*. It means to give into the hands of another; to give over into one's power or use; to deliver to one something to keep, use, or take care of (manage). Jesus exemplified this as He spoke quite frequently of the fact that He came to do exactly what the Father had sent Him to do and carried out every detail to perfection. Jesus' preparation extended directly from His complete trust in God. He received His assignment from God. Who else would He trust in? Trust is something far more than a verbal indication but is expressed by a willingness to be compliant and seeing it through. You must understand that when you don't trust in the one who sent you, you sway away from your instructions and try to accomplish the assignment on your own. Parents, don't you have this same problem with your children? Either they think that they just flat out know better, you don't understand, or know what you're talking about, so they just venture off and go about it on their own. Jesus didn't do this. He trusted the Father to the very point of death. As a matter of fact, He always followed the example set by the Father (John 5:19). There's no doubt that Jesus had a very unique relationship with God that was consistent twenty-four hours a day, seven days a week. He was God Himself, so you can't get any more unique than that. This relationship afforded Him the ability to consistently stay connected with and rely upon God. When His time had drawn near, Jesus' reliance upon God intensified. Just before Jesus was arrested, back in the Garden of Gethsemane, we find Him full of sorrow. He went straight to the one whom He knew could help. He prayed earnestly to God. Once? Twice? No, He repeated the process three times. He would not continue on without consulting the wisdom of and gaining the strength He needed from God to get through His dilemma. Now, take a look at your own life and contemplate your own tendencies. How close do you come to lean on God? Being that we are not as uniquely connected to God as Jesus is, how much more motivated should we be in gaining access to God in our times of trouble? Also, in a parallel account leading up to His arrest, Jesus is found praying on behalf of others (John 17:6-26). Knowing that His time to leave this world is steadily approaching, Jesus is concerned about how that will affect His disciples and all believers that would come after them. He prays to God for their protection. Interestingly, He prayed not for their protection from the physical harm that will be exerted on them by the world, but for their unity together. He prayed that it would mirror the unity that He has with the Father. What was of extreme importance is that they would not become like the rest of the world again. Often times, when we are facing trials, we aren't aware of how our experiences may impact those who are the closest to us. We are so caught up in ourselves and focused on how we're going to get through our situation. When you trust in God, you don't have to be consumed with the "what am I going to do" type of attitude because it is already laid out there for you. All you have to do is search His manual for the answers. It frees you up to be more outwardly focused because it is no longer just your situation, but God's as well. This is a change of mind that I must incorporate into my life. I'm just not accustomed to the idea of having a Father who wants to help me through my trials and hold my arms up when I am weak. So, most often with me, my initial thought is not to always pray when facing challenging times. It's more like the afterthought. My view of authority figures is tainted in that all they do is bark commands for you to follow and wait to scold you when you fall short. They say to do this and do that, and it's up to me to comply or else. This is a result of my interaction with authority figures during my childhood. Leadership and having authority is so different from this. Jesus used His authority and leadership to serve others. One of the amazing things about God is that He wants to help you with all of the things in your life that drive you crazy. Why? For starters, it's because He loves and cares for you very deeply (I Peter 5:6-7). And two, He can handle whatever it is and you can't. It's as simple as that. After Jesus informed His disciples of the bad news of His departure (John 13:33), He reassures them of the key ingredient for endurance. He said, "Do not let your hearts be troubled. Trust in God; trust also in me (John 14:1)."

Thinking about the next suggestion, I must admit that it really hits close to home with me. As I reminisce about my life experiences, I think about the missed opportunities and my reluctance to try new experiences because I was so apprehensive. Many of us pass on from this life not getting anywhere near the most out of our years here. I know you've heard this probably thousands of times, maybe millions depending on how old you are, but life is *way too* short (added *way too* for a little variety and some emphasis). Being a Christian, I am reminded of one of Jesus' purposes for coming. He said that He came so that they may have life and have it to the full (John 10:10). Jesus is specifically talking about those who are His true followers evidenced by their submission and obedience to Him as sheep are with their shepherd (v1-10). How this was accomplished lies in the depth of verse 11. The good shepherd lays down His life for the sheep. You see, we're back to that suffering idea again. Let's briefly take a look at something else for a moment to really hit the point. An aspect of God's character is that He is a long-suffering god. This is apparent by His patience in waiting for lost souls to come to the knowledge of the truth, repent, and be reconciled. For thousands of years since the fall of man, God watched His creation rebel against Him as we drowned in our cesspool of sin without so much as an ounce of regret. Even after all of that, He still rescues mankind by giving His only Son over to death with the full knowledge that the majority of mankind will elect to pass on this very precious gift. This, God did all out of His great and inexplicable love for us simply because He is love (Romans 5:6-8, I John 4:9-10). And, don't think for a minute that it stops there. True Christians continue to cause God pain as we embark on and progress in the Christian lifestyle being torn between living by the Spirit and living according to our flesh which is why Paul warns the Ephesians against grieving the Holy Spirit of God. This is the very battle that he is describing when he wrote to the disciples in Rome (Romans 7:14-21). After thinking about all of this, I believe that it is safe to say that there is some degree or element of pain and suffering in love that we should come to expect. It is a natural part of the process. I feel that we miss out on the greater things in life, the living life to the fullest that Jesus brought because we are so reluctant or flat out refuse to be vulnerable. This is especially visible in our relationships with one another. We don't love each other the way we should because that requires us to give dangerously more of ourselves. It opens us up to the possibility of being hurt more frequently and deeper. We are called to follow the example of Jesus in every aspect of our lives. This one is no different. We need to grow in our ability to be more vulnerable with God and with each other. In his relationship with God, I can't think of a man more vulnerable and more transparent than David. His relationship with God was remarkable. Have you read his Psalms? David was very expressive with God about his joy, his pain, his sorrow, his sin, his trials, his weaknesses. On many occasions, I got the impression that he was on an emotional roller coaster – one minute, God was his rock, his fortress, and was going to protect him from all harm. The next minute, he was hopeless and destined to fall into the hands of his enemies. In today's society, that kind of behavior is considered to be so distant from being a man. It is looked upon as being weak, but I'd be willing to bet that you wouldn't have told David that to his face. We are so proficient at putting on this façade of being impenetrable, disguising our feelings, or disconnecting from them altogether. We do this in an effort to protect ourselves from being hurt. The logic in this is that I've been hurt by past experiences, so I'm not going to give as much the next time. I can't think of a situation where this is more evident than our relationship with the opposite sex. Women are so frustrated with their husbands because they are not vulnerable. They just won't let them in. Dating relationships suffer because men and women alike are afraid to give of themselves because of experiences in previous dating relationships. People hold grudges against an entire race or the opposite sex because of something that one person from that group did to them. The rationale is that, if one of them is like that, then they all must be like that. The absurdity in that thinking has long gone unnoticed. But, I must confess my guilt in this area as well. It is by far too blatantly obvious to pass by. Shortly, before I became a Christian, I remember being at my apartment with this girl I was seeing at the time. She was in the kitchen while I was in the living room watching television. I guess I had a moment where I went into deep thought as I do sometimes and emerged with an epiphany about my lapse in being more giving to my girlfriend or something like that. I, then, remember speaking to her saying, "I just don't do the things that I used to do in previous relationships." She immediately responded, "Oh, that's natural", like it was no big deal at all. Months later, after we stopped seeing each other, I thought about that conversation and became rather appalled. First, by what my statement was really saying underneath. In essence, I was saying that I was treating her less or giving her less of myself than I did others before her due to hurt I experienced with those that preceded her. Secondly, I think that I was even more shocked by her response. According to her response and the tone of her voice, it was totally acceptable. I thought that I absolutely wouldn't want anyone treating me any less because of something someone else did to them. That's punishing one person for something another person has done, so to speak. That's the issue I had with the girl I dated just before her. She tried to pay me back for every bad thing that every guy before me had done to her. Then, I turn around and did the same thing to this other girl. Although it wasn't my intention, that really doesn't matter in the end. The damage it can have on a relationship is exactly the same.

I have another story that I'd like to share in regard to this, but regarding a whole different situation. See if this situation sounds familiar to you. I'm in a situation where I get to see a particular woman almost on a daily basis. I found this woman to be very attractive from the moment that I first saw her. As I began to take note of her personality, she seemed to be very nice and genuine. I don't know about you, but in my book, this easily bumped her up to extremely attractive. My interest peaked to the point of wanting to get to know her, and for the longest time, I had wanted to ask her out to lunch. Of course, it would be my treat. Frankly, I didn't ask her because I was rather intimidated. Some months had passed by, and this was beginning to eat me up. At times I found myself thinking what if she would go and we hit it off, but I would never know. Other times, I found myself looking in her general direction just to catch a glimpse of her. She became a distraction to me, but not in a bad way and at no fault other than my own. As I had been sharing with my roommate what had been going on with me, I told him one day that I was going to ask her out. I realized that I needed to do this. I had to get resolved about it in my heart and, by now, it was painfully obvious that it wasn't going to go away like I had thought it would. So, the very next opportunity that I had, I mustered up the courage to talk to her about it. It turned out that she currently had a boyfriend. We had a nice, short conversation. It was good. Afterward, I was able to move on. For the entire time leading up to my decision to speak with her, I had made up excuses as to why I shouldn't ask her – she had a boyfriend, she won't date a younger guy, etc. I ran through them all. I had realized that what was at the heart of my issue was the fact that I didn't want to be vulnerable. I didn't want to entrust myself in the hands of another, especially someone I didn't know. What if this woman embarrasses me? What if she blatantly dogs me out? What if she belittles me? That was the real issue that I was dealing with. Don't get me wrong; it's not that what I was thinking wasn't a possibility. To varying degrees, we can be pretty merciless, especially when we know we have the upper hand on someone. In reality, I had no idea or way of knowing if that would happen in that situation or any other as a matter of fact. But, if I wasn't willing to take the risk, I would have never known. I would have avoided the potentially hurtful situation, but also would have avoided the potential blessing in the process. Like many other situations in life we face, if we aren't willing to take the risk (not senseless ones, mind you), we will never, ever get what we want out of life. Although she did have a boyfriend, we ended up having an encouraging conversation. From that experience, I learned that living life to the fullest doesn't mean getting everything you want or having everything go your way all of the time. It simply means having experiences that benefit us and allow us to grow so that we can appreciate and enjoy life so much more than we would have without them. In order to achieve this fulfillment, we must learn and strive to overcome our fear of being vulnerable where necessary. This doesn't mean being hard-hearted acting as though you don't feel anything, couldn't care less, and that nothing affects you. That's on the other end of the spectrum and is just as damaging or ineffective. If you feel or think this way, then you're one of those merciless people that I spoke of earlier. You are the type of person that makes it difficult for those who are more vulnerable. God created us to be emotional beings. It's how we are able to connect and have great relationships with God as well as each other. As I hinted to earlier, our relationships suffer when we decide not to feel or give of ourselves. We pretty much become like a brick or an inanimate object when interacting with others. We make it virtually impossible for people to connect with us. Whether by our inability, our unwillingness, or our ignorance, many of us, especially men, have hurt someone or damaged a relationship by our lack of connecting to the other individual involved. In order for us to get the most out of life and our relationships, we must be willing to be vulnerable and risk the possibility of being hurt. It all boils down to this. We have to decide what's most important to us. Are you going to be reluctant to give of yourself, be guarded, and overly protective of yourself and live in mediocrity? Or, are you willing to be vulnerable, be a risk-taker, and live life to the fullest the way Jesus desires for us? Moreover, this is what hinders us from being fully led by God because being led by God means going places we don't naturally want to go and doing things we don't naturally want to do (John 21:18-19). This takes an unbelievable amount of vulnerability and submission. Unfortunately, these attributes present a constant battle for us. Yielding ourselves to any degree to another is simply unheard of. It's in stark contrast to our nature. We desire to have control, and this prevents us from being our very best for God because it's truly about how much we allow ourselves to be used by God, not about how much we can do for God. Do you see this quality in the message of the cross? Consider the possibility of this for a moment. What if Jesus was more concerned about the fact that He was innocent and that His treatment was undeserved? What if He responded the way we do when we're in similar situations? We probably wouldn't have much of a gospel now, would we?

As an introduction to my last suggestion, think about this for a moment. Have you ever had an activity or been a part of something that gave you a great sense of purpose, fulfillment, or served as a means of escape? For whatever reason it may be, whether personal or its worthiness, this activity commanded your undivided attention so much that, once engaged, there aren't many things that can divert your attention. Its significance to you literally dwarfs any competition. I believe that we all have things in life that capture our hearts to the degree that we just lose ourselves within them. With the same fire and arousal of passion, I believe that we must give ourselves over to God's purposes. When we immerse ourselves in the service of God, we are, in a sense, alleviated from a lot of the pain and suffering we experience in this world. This doesn't mean that we escape altogether, but we are freed from being weighed down excessively by the burden because we are not so focused on the catastrophic event we are undergoing. This is very similar in point to our transgressions and following the law (Galatians 5:1). In Christ, believers are released from the Old Testament law so that they can have the freedom to truly love and serve God along with others (Galatians 5:13). The focus or object of love and servitude is never oneself, but always the other individual. Without this taking place, we'd be a bunch of overly burdened, self-focused people with no hope of ever-changing or having peace because we don't have the power to free ourselves (Romans 5:6-10). We'd literally be consumed with our own disposition before God in every little thing we did. My point doesn't intend for us to neglect altogether those matters that we need to tend to or that we shouldn't be grieved by matters such as the sudden loss or chronic illness of a loved one, a family member being called into duty, or some other tragic event, you fill in the blanks. What I'm saying is there is a myriad of things that we give far too much attention to – way more than they deserve. For example, how many of you have gotten into a heated argument with your spouse, friend, or whomever only to forget moments later what you were arguing about in the first place? This is assuming that you knew what you were fighting about to begin with. It's just better that we don't give too much attention to some matters because they aren't good for us. The things of this world are so temporary, yet we are in the habit of giving them a far greater significance than they're worth. On the contrary, the purposes of God are so noble, worthy, and have eternal value. His purposes are always meant to take precedence in our lives, even in the midst of trials.

> ³This is good, and pleases God our Savior, ⁴who wants all men to be saved and to come to a knowledge of the truth. ⁵For there is one God and one mediator between God and men, the man Christ Jesus, ⁶who gave himself as a ransom for all men – the testimony given in its proper time. ⁷And for this purpose I was appointed a herald and an apostle – I am telling the truth, I am not lying – and a teacher of the true faith to the Gentiles.
>
> (I Timothy 2:3-7)

God's greatest desire is that all of mankind will come to a knowledge of the truth and escape the impending doom that every man is destined for (Ezekiel 18:30-32). This means of escape is the news that must be broadcast to every eardrum around the globe. It is with this priceless piece of information that Christians are to utilize in duplicating themselves and is the foundation of the lifelong process of spiritual maturation. This entire process was the final command by our Lord before He ascended into heaven (Matthew 28:18-20). If you're not sharing the good news, then, how will those you are capable of reaching ever hear? If you're not maturing spiritually, how will those you are capable of reaching ever see a difference in your life? This is what Paul said he was appointed a herald of. If you know anything about his life, you know that he lived up to this appointment through some of the worst of circumstances. God has appointed all of those who proclaim Christianity to be heralds of the only real good news there is in life once you remove all of the meaningless clutter that we get so preoccupied with. Paul journeyed across great distances eagerly preaching the gospel of Jesus Christ to cities who may not have heard. He penned letters from prison to fellow Christians to assist them in their spiritual maturation and to encourage them in their hardships. Paul was driven by this call. Unfortunately, in our day, many Christians neglect to incorporate this clear command of our Lord into their lives regularly. I must admit that many times I haven't been as passionate about sharing the good news as I should or had been on other occasions. Once diagnosed, this is an illness that requires immediate repentance. Although Paul was driven by his purpose, there was never or ever will be a man so purposed towards His mission than Jesus Christ. In order to reach His goal, He faced a full circle of trials and tribulations ranging from resistance by His own family to multiple attempts on His life. Ironically, His goal was to get to the cross. The cross, which separated Him from the Father, was the greatest suffering He would experience and the ultimate price He would pay on our behalf. Jesus suffered spiritually, physically, and emotionally in going to the cross. When His cousin was wrongly thrown into prison, Jesus began fulfilling His purpose. He went out to preach and called His first disciples (Matthew 4:12-22, Mark 1:14-20). I'm quite sure that Jesus cared about His cousin very much. It's just that He had a higher purpose to fulfill and it would do very little to run to John's rescue. As Jesus forewarned, deserved or undeserved, there's going to be trouble in this world. For most of us, our handling of this type of situation would have gone very differently. We would have neglected to choose what was better. Jesus conveys this same message to Martha while visiting her home (Luke 10:38-42). When we elect to take the path that Mary chose, choosing what is better, we display our willingness to trust in God that He will work things out the way they need to be. This results in being able to be at peace in some of the worst of circumstances. I learned this lesson during the separation from my ex-wife through a basketball league that I started running at the beginning of 2007. This league wasn't your ordinary league that you'd find in your local community centers. This league was created with the specific purpose of sharing the gospel of Jesus Christ. It was designed to serve as an outreach tool to help those who would come to Christ. As the year transitioned from 2006 to 2007, I had been playing consistently in three basketball leagues per week with a little pick-up ball on Sunday evenings. Neither of these leagues was located anywhere near the neighborhood where I lived. As a matter of fact, two were completely across town, and the other was located out of town. In these leagues, you had one game which lasted approximately an hour long, if you were lucky. So, it's not like I was playing a lot of basketball when I went. On top of that, I had to share playing time with others. One night, while waiting for my game to begin, I was watching the previous game. As I looked around at everybody, it dawned on me that people who play basketball love to play some basketball. For even a minimal amount of time, they will travel great distances to play in basketball leagues. Shoot, I was living proof of that all by myself. I thought that it would be great to have a league where we prefix each game with a devotional and prayer. We would penalize profanity and fighting in an effort to create a respectful, courteous, and peaceful environment indicative of one that would glorify God. This would give individuals the chance to hear and respond to the good news of Jesus that would otherwise not have had the chance to hear it. Being that I was introduced to my church through a one-time basketball league it hosted in 2000, which led me to become a disciple of Jesus, I thought that this was definitely an excellent idea. After finding out that some in church leadership were onboard, we took the idea and ran with it. Since its inauguration, there have been two young men who have decided to follow Jesus and became baptized disciples. There have been others who have visited my church or one of the many bible talks we have around town. I even caught wind of the fact that the referees were specifically requesting to work the games in our league. But, most importantly, many are hearing the gospel of Jesus on a regular basis. There's a different person each week who volunteers to come out to lead the devotionals and time of prayer for each game. We've had sessions of the league where the content of the devotional from week to week was open to whatever was on the devotional leader's heart but geared towards meeting the need of non-disciples. Lately, for each session, we've had them centered on a theme that built upon the content from week to week. A couple of recent themes are "Who is God? – His Attributes, His Personality", which centered on, of course, the personality and character traits of God and what they mean for each of us. Now, we are doing "Touched by Christ", which is a character study of some individuals from the Bible as they were transformed by their interaction with Jesus Christ. This theme is meant to convey the fact that you can't be a follower of Jesus and be the same person you were before you met Him. Although there are a number of disciples who play in the league from session to session, the devotionals are catered to appeal to those who are not disciples and designed with the intent of pricking their hearts and prompting them to question the activities of their lives. In more ways than one, the league has definitely made an impact on those who have been involved. As you may have been able to gather, this league has been very beneficial to me as well. Not only has it served as a distraction during my hardships in the form of providing me something more meaningful to focus on, but it has also helped me to find my niche in God's kingdom. Being able to take a gift, talent, or ability, especially something you love and use it to serve God should be at the heart of every disciple. This is simply our gift back to God. It's an expression of our appreciation to Him for the inexpressible greatness He has lavished upon us. This basketball league has been just that for me. It hasn't been without its challenges and discouraging moments but remember that anything worthwhile having will not be complete without its share of trials.

No More Pain

The time that I spent in Las Vegas, Nevada living with my dad was by far the most traumatic experience in my life.

Being that I was at a point in my life where I was developing into the person I would become as an adult, I think that a lot of my character took shape from the experiences that I had during this period. How I view life, myself, and the people around me was definitely impacted negatively. From time to time, I've wondered how I would have been different if I hadn't experienced such a tragedy. While living there, I knew that my mother was doing all that she could to get me back. As time went on, the situation began to look bleak. I felt so hopeless in regard to my predicament. On different occasions, I thought about running away from home. This was especially true the Christmas morning when my dad threw me into the wall for the second time. I left and stayed away from home the entire day. I was angry, and I didn't want to go back. But, in the end, I eventually did. Even as an adult, I've occasionally found myself speculating as to why I didn't just leave. Who knows? It may have been best that I stayed. But, I do believe that I felt as though I didn't have anywhere to go for help. I thought I would end up right back there with him only to be beaten worse for trying to leave. People do see things, and I know there were people that knew something fishy was going on at my house. The guy that lived across the street from me told me that he and his parents knew something was going on at my house. This made me wonder what they had seen and why they didn't call for help. With the loss of hope and motivation, I concluded that my only hope of getting out would be when I turned eighteen. I would be able to go to college and just disappear as far as they would have been concerned. I had already begun to think that maybe I would just transfer schools or something without them knowing. The only catch was to make it through alive the eight years that I had left to get to that point. Thank God that He had another plan for getting me out much sooner than I expected because

I sure didn't want to go through another eight or nine more years of that.

In April of 1982, I was a sixth-grader at Jim Bridger Jr. High School. One morning, I was at my locker prior to my first-period class. My locker was located on the back hallway, not far from the entrance that led outside of the building. As I glanced towards the exit, I happened to see a very familiar woman walk past the doorway. Immediately, I looked up towards the exit again and thought, "That woman looks just like my mother." It crossed my mind to go take a closer look, but I thought that it couldn't possibly be her. So, I continued to grab what I needed and rushed off to Ms. Halloway's class. Shortly after I got to class, a voice over the intercom requested that I come to the office because my mother was waiting for me. Thinking that it was my dad's wife, I angrily thought to myself, "What does this white woman want?" My intention is that no one takes offense to this remark or thinks that I'm a racist or something. This is not the case. I'm only being real and sharing exactly what I was thinking at the time. If anyone has taken offense, please accept my apologies. As I proceeded to go to the office, I continued to grumble. I muttered, "She has no right posing as my mother! She's not my mother! Who does she think she is?" The woman that I saw while standing at my locker never, ever crossed my mind. When I arrived in the office, my eyes panned back and forth across the office. But, I didn't see who I was expecting to see. Suddenly, someone unexpected caught my eye from the far side of the office. It was my mother; she had come to take me back home. My jaw dropped, and my eyes bulged out of my head because I was so shocked to see her. I realized then that it was her that I had seen earlier. She beckoned me to follow her out the back door of the office. No one in the office knew what was going on. It's fortunate that my dad's wife had never been up to the school. I walked calmly over to the other side of the office and made my way towards the exit. The office had a very large glass that allowed you to see outside. Having her thinking cap on and knowing that this would be an emotional reunion that would cause those in the office to be alarmed, she walked up the walkway a bit so that no one in the office could see and waited for me. Once I got outside that door, I immediately took off my Oakland A's batter's hat, threw it to the ground, and raced to my mother's arms. As we embraced, we began to cry tears of joy. I held her so tight. I felt as though I didn't want to let her go. There aren't any words that could capture the totality of that moment. My eyes well up with tears now as I am moved by just the thought of it. Far from my mind were the physical beatings, verbal abuse, belittlement, and other maltreatments that caused me so much pain, anguish, and suffering. It was like it never existed. All I knew was I was free, and I was going back home where I belonged. My mother went back to pick up the hat that I left in front of the office window. Then, we walked away hand in hand. As we talked, I was somewhat in disbelief and remember just looking up at her and all I could do was smile. It was so amazing how God worked all of that out. If you're a Christian, He has something in store for us that's beyond the description of words.

Similarly, the church in Thessalonica was undergoing its share of trials in the form of persecution. The church was young and had a lot of young disciples. It was imperative that they received encouragement to endure through the trials they were facing. The persecution was so severe that it caused Paul and Silas to leave in a hurry under the cover of the night (Acts 17:1-10). When Paul wrote the first letter to the Thessalonians to encourage them, he ended every chapter of the letter with a reference to the second coming of Jesus Christ. The most descriptive of those references come from the fourth chapter.

> [13]Brothers, we do not want you to be ignorant about those who fall asleep, or to grieve like the rest of men, who have no hope. [14]We believe that Jesus died and rose again and so we believe that God will bring with Jesus those who have fallen asleep in him. [15]According to the

> Lord's own word, we tell you that we who are still alive, who are left till the coming of the Lord, will certainly not precede those who have fallen asleep. [16]For the Lord himself will come down from heaven, with a loud command, with the voice of the archangel and with the trumpet call of God, and the dead in Christ will rise first. [17]After that, we who are still alive and are left will be caught up together with them in the clouds to meet the Lord in the air. And so we will be with the Lord forever. [18]Therefore encourage each other with these words.
>
> (I Thessalonians 4:13-18)

I love this passage of Scripture for the imagery it presents of our coming family reunion. Notice that Paul didn't tell them how to avoid their trials or pray for their removal. Instead, he gave them a specific point in time to focus on. What was the significance of Paul making all of those references to Jesus' second coming to the Thessalonians? Paul motivated them with this because he didn't want them to lose hope. Without this hope, they would have no reason to continue in their faith through the trials they were facing. It was repeated so frequently because he wanted it to stick in their minds. Sometimes, saying something just once doesn't do the job. In the same way, we must think of Jesus' return as often as possible because if we don't, what motivation is there left to keep us from letting go of our faith when trials and suffering comes? For disciples of Jesus, our suffering is not going to last forever. This is centered on Jesus' second coming. Can you imagine the immense amount of joy and excitement? Similar to when I embraced my mother at our reunion, all of the things that brought you pain and suffering will no longer exist to you. It will be as if it never, ever happened. Imagine being a part of this spectacular event. Allow your imagination to run away with it. Can you imagine walking on the air? What about seeing the sky filled with millions upon millions of your spiritual brothers and sisters? Many of those will have served before you. There will be many that you've served with side by side. And, many will be those who replaced you when your time was up. But now, we all will be together as one big happy family making our way to the One who made it all possible. So often, many of us pray that God takes the suffering away. But, more appropriately, we should be praying that we would endure in such a way that His purposes will be fulfilled in our lives through the suffering. Jesus has already promised us a place and a time where there will be no more suffering. That time is not now. So, keep enduring through the storms because just on the other side of those dark clouds, the Son is waiting to shine His glory on you. Amen!

REFERENCES

1 Lawlor, Christopher. September 22, 2005. "Nose Tackle Has Special Abilities." USA Today. Retrieved 2007 (http://www.usatoday.com/sports/preps/football/2005-09-22-martin_x.htm

2 Peet, Dr. Mary, NCSU. "Sustainable Practices for Vegetable Production in the South." Retrieved 2007 (http://www.ncsu.edu/sustainable/profiles/harv_tom.html),

3 "Somali Pirates Drown With Share of Ransom from Sirius Star Hijack." Guardian.co.uk. January 10, 2009. Retrieved January 2009 (http://www.guardian.co.uk/world/2009/jan/10/sirius-star-somalia-pirates-drown).

4 Levenson, Michael. July 23, 2008. "Facing Foreclosure, Tanton Woman Commits Suicide." The Boston Globe. Retrieved January 2009 (http://www.boston.com/news/local/breaking_news/2008/07/facing_foreclos.html).

5 Boston, William. January 6, 2009. "Why Adolf Merclke Killed Himself?" Time. Retrieved January 2009 (http://www.time.com/time/business/article/0,8599,1870007,00.html?iid=digg_share).

6 Binkley, Christina. May 29, 2008. "The 'Sex' Effect: Empowering To Some, Trashy to Others." The Wall Street Journal. Retrieved September 27, 2009 (http://online.wsj.com/article/SB121201752162527645.html).

7 Shah, Priya Florence. September 4, 2006. "Stupid Mistake #3: Using Sex as a Weapon." Soul Kadee. Retrieved September 9, 2009 (http://www.soulkadee.com/2006/09/04/stupid-mistake-3-using-sex-as-a-weapon).

8 Aberra, Dr. Tseday. April 22, 2008. "Using Sex as a Weapon and the Other Six Biggest Mistakes Married Women Make." Reuters. Retrieved September 27, 2009 (http://www.reuters.com/article/pressRelease/idUS211611+22-Apr-2008+MW20080422).

9 Popenoe, David. 2002. "The Top Ten Myths of Divorce." Rutgers. Retrieved September 9, 2009 (http://marriage.rutgers.edu/Publications/pubtoptenmyths.htm).

www.ingramcontent.com/pod-product-compliance
Lightning Source LLC
LaVergne TN
LVHW091532060526
838200LV00036B/579